"The distinguishing characteristic of a traditional folk game is that although it has rules they are not written. Nobody knows exactly what they are. The players have a tradition to guide them, but must settle among themselves the details of how to play a particular game."

From **ONE POTATO, TWO POTATO:**
The SECRET EDUCATION of AMERICAN CHILDREN,
by Mary and Herbert Knapp.

"Well, perhaps you haven't found it so yet," said Alice; "but when you have to turn into a chrysalis - you will some day you know - and then after that into a butterfly, I should think you'll feel it a little queer, won't you?"

"Not a bit," said the Caterpillar.

"Well, perhaps *your* feelings may be different," said Alice: "all I know is, it would feel very queer to *me*."

"You!" said the Caterpillar contemptuously. "Who are *you*?"

From **ALICE'S ADVENTURES in WONDERLAND,**
by Lewis Carroll.

the
SANDMAN
a game of you

WRITTEN BY
NEIL GAIMAN

ILLUSTRATED BY
SHAWN McMANUS
COLLEEN DORAN
BRYAN TALBOT
GEORGE PRATT
STAN WOCH
DICK GIORDANO

LETTERED BY
TODD KLEIN

COLORED BY
DANNY VOZZO

COVERS BY
DAVE McKEAN

INTRODUCED BY
SAMUEL R. DELANY

FEATURING CHARACTERS CREATED BY
NEIL GAIMAN, SAM KIETH, MIKE DRINGENBERG

the SANDMAN:
A GAME OF YOU

Published by DC Comics.
Cover and compilation Copyright © 2011
DC Comics. All Rights Reserved. Introduction
Copyright © 1993 DC Comics. All Rights
Reserved.

Originally published
in single magazine issues
as SANDMAN 32-37.
Copyright © 1991, 1992 DC Comics.
All Rights Reserved.

DC Comics. 1700 Broadway, New York, NY 10019
A Warner Bros. Entertainment Company.

Printed in the USA. Fourth Printing.
ISBN: 978-1-4012-3043-2

Cover art, interior illustrations and
publication design by Dave McKean.

Cover design by Richard Bruning.

SUSTAINABLE FORESTRY INITIATIVE

Certified Chain of Custody
At Least 20% Certified Forest Content
www.sfiprogram.org
SFI-01042
APPLIES TO TEXT STOCK ONLY

Library of Congress Cataloging-in-Publication Data

Gaiman, Neil.
  The sandman : a game of you / writer, Neil Gaiman; pencils, Shawn
McManus.
    p. cm.
  "Originally published in single magazine form as The Sandman 32-37."
  ISBN 978-1-4012-3043-2 (softcover)
  1. Graphic novels. I. McManus, Shawn. II. Title.
  PN6728.S26G36 2011
  741.5'973—dc22
                    2011008842

SKERRIES *of the* DREAM

A PREFACE BY
SAMUEL R. DELANY

So the first thing I did was turn to the Oxford English Dictionary and look up "skerry," where I found:

A rugged, insulated sea-rock or stretch of rocks, covered by the sea at high water or in stormy weather;
a reef.

It's quite a resonant image, those distant, only partially visible solidities, now and again drowned in dreams —temporarily lost in them. Neil Gaiman plays with it elegantly in the writing; and Shawn McManus (as do Colleen Doran, Bryan Talbot, and Stan Woch) plays with it equally elegantly in the drawings.

THE SANDMAN is one of the most popular comics of our day—and popular with the oddest lot of people. We're all used to the idea of comic books resonating with elemental mythic patterns: the late lamented Superman, the currently thriving Batman, and Wonder Woman. But, when all is said and done, as such myths go, they're pretty brutal things. THE SANDMAN, under the writerly direction of Gaiman, does its work delicately, probing in areas where, often, we might not even have suspected anything mythical lay. It explores always with an ironic cast to the lips. The eyes are narrowed. The approach is always skewed.

Again and again, what it discovers shocks, chills, catches at the heart. It sends us to strange places, to the most distant shores of the imaginative, the mystical, to explore the stuff that can only be figured in dreams...

To talk about these tales in too much more detail, let me warn you, I will have to talk about the plot—what happens in them. Those of you who haven't read them before might better go on and read them now. The analysis that follows will be more fun for a reader already familiar with them. And some of that fun might be, for some of you, spoiled by the odd, upcoming revelation.

Gaiman's **A Game of You**—this particular Sandman series—begins in the snow: need we note that for the comics colorist, depicting snow requires the minimum amount of ink? Take a look: Color there is all but restricted to the shading over the caption boxes. (And that color says: look at the *language* in this tale...) What we have in the opening three pages is two streams of information, all but unconnected, one verbal, one visual. The visual one, by the bottom of the first page, has become shocking: a desiccated corpse!

At the same time the words provide a strangely distanced, even elegant, colloquy between speakers named Prinado and Luz, about the Cuckoo, the Princess, and the Tantoblin—carrying us right past that shock, into the second page, toward a spot of black: a hole in the snow—a hole, a blackness, that grows larger and larger, till, by the bottom of page three, it engulfs the reader, filling its panel.

Need we note that an all-black panel requires the *most* ink possible from the comics inker? (The only color there is restricted to the shading over the caption boxes: look at the language.). But here two eyes blink in that darkness, to look, indeed, in the direction of the words...

What's happening in this three-page prologue is that we are given two simultaneous worlds, as it were, both highly subjective, one represented by words, one represented by pictures. Both are highly formalized—the one represented by words through the deeply conventionalized diction associated with high fantasy, the one represented by pictures through the formal progression from white to black. Both contain violences.

The shocks in one information stream—the starkly drawn ribs of the corpse at the bottom of page one, the verbal shock of "The Tantoblin will not come. I felt him die. The Black Guard found him in the night," even as they fall within the same panel—jar one another; as we move our attention back and forth between one stream and the other, there is impingement, distortion, and interaction that all but obliterates the distinctions the formalities set in place. And that—in case you're wondering—in spite of the abstract language, is a description of what is going to go on through the rest of **A Game of You.**

It's our opening example of how the game will be played:

Two worlds—and elements from each will constantly impinge, cross over, to shock and distort what goes on in the other.

Also, we're going to get, just incidentally, a tale that covers just about the range of what comics can do—from panels almost pure white to panels almost pure black.

The way to become really frustrated with **A Game of You** is, however, to read one world as reality, the world of Barbie, Wanda, Hazel and Foxglove, and one world as fantasy: the world of Prinado, Luz, Wilkinson, and the Cuckoo. If you try to read one as a simple allegory for the other—if you look in one for a extensional explanation of the other—you will not be a happy camper. Clive Barker, in his introduction to **The Doll's House**, noted that Gaiman's tales tend to take place not in a world where fantasy invades the real, but rather in what Barker called a "far more delirious" form: "In these narratives, the whole world is haunted and mysterious. There is no solid status quo, only a series of relative realities, personal to each of the characters, any and all of which are frail, and subject to eruptions from other states and conditions." The visual shock that comes as the reader leaves page three of **A Game of You** to turn to page four—the transition from the snow-and-shadow world of the Land, where death is an ugly splatter of ink at the bottom of the page in the progression from white to black, to the sheer *messiness* of Barbie's room (a chaos of clothing and wall photos and rumpled bedding wholly organized around the sexuality of Barbie's buns, incidentally) immediately suggests this *is* going to be a two-tiered fantasy, of the real and the imagined.

But hold on to Barker's point. He's been there before…

Consider: in the world that we—certainly—*start* to read as real, the sullen top-floor neighbor harbors a horde of malignant crows inside his rib cage; the quiet girl upstairs with the oversized glasses who drinks soy milk is hundreds of years old; here, it turns out, the moon *cares* whether or not you have a "y" chromosome, and punishes you accordingly. No, *this* is a fantasy world, too.

The world of THE SANDMAN finally takes its power from its intense saturation of irony. Here, the Lord of all Dream has a smart-alec crow for a sidekick called Matthew who calls his boss "boss." It's a world where a stuffed toy animal can scare an old homeless woman into a near heart attack—or betray you to the point of death. In THE SANDMAN a mourner draws the threads of a veil on her face in a restroom with an eyebrow pencil—and, because it's a comic book, we, the readers, can't tell the difference between it and a "real" veil—but all the characters can and comment on it constantly. ("What's that on your face?") It's a world where a "Wundabud" commercial (that's a brand of cotton swab) plays through a storm that all but destroys a neighborhood—in short, it's a world almost as heavily laced with ironies as our own.

The key to this fantasy is Wanda's troubling death (alongside the death of the single black character in the tale)-which drew a whole host of very concerned ideological criticism, when readers first encountered it in issue #36, part five. (And, I confess, Hazel's ignorance of the mechanics of female reproduction seemed to me something one would be more likely to find in the suburban heartland, even at the center on Barbie's Florida childhood—rather than on the third floor of a Lower East Side tenement. But the same reading applies...) Wanda's initial biological sex is of the same visual status as the aforementioned ironic black mourner's veil at the final Kansas funeral: the biologically naive (Hazel), as well as the forces of religion (Thessaly) and the family (Alvin's) now and again speak about it. But we, the readers, just can't *see* it. (The veil is simply *erased* at the end...) And because the comics are a fundamentally visual medium, that palpable invisibility may finally be the strongest statement the story has to make about the topic to the common (comics) reader. It seems to me, as I was saying, that the key to this particular fantasy world is precisely that it *is* a fantasy world where the natural forces, stated and unstated, whether of myth or of chance, *enforce* the dominant ideology we've got around us today, no matter what. (The dominant ideology is the collection of rules and regulations that includes, among many other things, the one that says that in popular narratives, like the *Dirty Harry* films, say, all the members of oppressed groups, blacks, women, Asians, gays, or what have you, have to be killed off at the end, no matter how good and noble they are—so that we can feel sorry for them, then forget about them. The dominant ideology is what's challenged by, among many other things, something like the ACT-UP slogan: "We're here. We're queer. We *won't* go way! Get used to us!") Making the supernatural forces in the tale the enforcers of the dominant ideology is what makes it a fantasy—and a rather nasty one at that.

And it remains just a nasty fantasy unless, in our reading of it, we can find some irony, something that subverts it, something that resists that fantasy, an array of details that turns the simple acceptance of that ideology into a problem—problematizes it, in Lit. Crit.-ese. But, as we said, almost everything in THE SANDMAN has its richness, its ironic spin. I'll mention a couple. But look for more. They're there. Taking the time to tease such subtleties out (and the problem with political readings is precisely that the large and general tend to overwhelm the subtle and specific) makes us stronger readers in the end, not because it makes us *excuse* such political patterns, but because we have to become even *more* sensitive to them, if we are to see how they are affected *by* the subtleties (which are, themselves, just as political).

In life, it will be the subtleties that start to wear away at the major social patterns of oppression, after all. It's the range of subtle subversions that set them up for the big changes that come by as better legislation, economic freedoms, and their material like.

(Notice when major social changes *are* finally legislated and formalized, they tend to surprise everyone *except* those who were paying attention to the details. That's why, in life and on the page, specific details are a good thing to pay attention to.)

Just as George's death (*he* will be called back to speak by Thessaly) will mirror Wilkinson's death (*he* will be called back to speak by Thessaly), Wanda's death at the end mirrors the Tantoblin's death at the beginning. What—? You don't know what sort of a goblin a Tantoblin is? Well, neither do I. What's more, the OED won't help us. (Though a "tanton" is an inmate of a hospital dedicated to St. Anthony...) The point is, as is made explicit in the dream in part one, Wanda doesn't really know who she is either. And since this has seldom been the problem of most of the would-be transsexuals of my acquaintance (if anything, it's quite the opposite), it's simply one more thing that weights the reading of this particular dream world toward a mode of the fantastic.

The question that **A Game of You** puts is: given a fantasy world in which, among other things, the dominant ideology is not socially constructed but is rather enforced by the transcendental order of nature, what will happen when an even wilder and more delirious order of fantasy is let loose in it?

It's a reasonable question, because, as we all know, one) people like Wanda's family, whom we will meet in part six, are quite convinced that God *is* precisely what keeps the dominant ideology in place and working, and, two) sometimes very bad things do happen to otherwise very nice, even heroic people—like Wanda.

So the tale is not without its relevance.

What is to be done?

For one, Barbie will be restricted to a nominal rebellion—which, perhaps, doesn't seem like much. The first rain will obliterate it, and likely no one in Kansas will ever know. But the idea of the nominal (in name only, having to do with names) is a big factor in **A Game of You.** While a name is always something *you* can choose, it only functions socially as long as I call you by it. (And try calling people names that they *don't* choose to be called by, if you want to see some real social unrest.) The power to choose one's own name is finally the major playing piece in the power game with which the story closes.

But let's look for a moment at another instance of parental naming in the story. Here's Wilkinson on *his* family's naming practices, during the journey through the Land, in part four:

I loved bein' a kid. I was one of seventeen children. We were all named Wilkinson—I suppose it was roughest on the girls, but we all got used to it in the end. I blame the parents, really... I would have liked to've bin an only child. That way when someone shouts Wilkinson, you know if it's you or not. Mustn't grumble. Our parents were the salt of the earth. Lovely people. It was just when they found a name they liked, they stuck with it.

In short, the Land is a fantasy world where there *is* no necessary distinction between male and female names for children—but, apparently, parents are just as sticky about preserving the name they pick as Wanda's parents turn out to be in part six. What we have here is an interesting satirical commentary, given in advance, on the closing moves of the game. (We won't even speculate on what prompted Barbie's parents to name *her*... And when she got together with her disastrous ex-boyfriend Ken, wasn't that just *too* cute...) This is not to say that life in the Land is all skittles and Courvoisier. The god the Land is sacred to is "Murphy," which, before we find out *his* real name, suggests nothing so much as the Murphy of Murphy's Law—that most pessimistic of observations on the Human Condition: "Anything that possibly *can* go wrong, will."

But there're other interesting correspondences between the two levels of fantasy. *Take* the idea of "cute." In Gaiman's fantasy New York, "cute" is Hazel and Foxglove's "cute frog mug" in which Wanda, utterly against all her own social and aesthetic leanings ("This?" she says to George, passing him on the stairs. "Oh, don't worry. It's not *my* cute frog mug. I'm carrying it for a friend."), must take the milk down for Barbie's coffee.

In the Land, however, being "cute" is the very survival mechanism of the Cuckoo—the principle of evil. Says the Cuckoo to Barbie, in their part-five encounter: "I've got a right to live, haven't I? And to be happy? ...And I'm awful sweet, aren't I. I'm *awful* cute." And Barbie's capitulation comes with the admission: "You're...cute...as a...button." From here, if we turn back to Wanda's encounter in part one with George on the stairs—George, with his crows, is, after all, an agent of the Cuckoo (who, once again, survives because the cute, the kitschy, the aesthetically impoverished and hopelessly sentimental hide her murderous impulses toward the stuff of fantasy that she appropriates by moving into the fantasies of others)—suddenly that encounter is given a second-reading resonance, a resonance, finally, essential to what Gaiman, I suspect, is all about in his SANDMAN stories...

For all we can get out of a careful rereading of Gaiman, the immediate pleasures of these stories to the first-time reader are many. It's the rare reader who does not respond to Gaiman's imaginative breadth, coupled with his simple accuracy of observation. The guarded caring with which his characters live with one another ("Don't take too much," Hazel warns Wanda, giving her the milk for Barbie's coffee) is comic and winning—and, of course, wholly recognizable. But this is a largely linear, melodic pleasure. There is also, however, a harmonic pleasure that accrues as detail resonates with detail. It is a pleasure that increases with careful, multiple readings. It is what makes these stories, in a word, art.

Gaiman's delirious world is held together always by relationships. Nor is his a world of relationships between fixed, solid egos, sure of them-"selves" and clear in their "identity." Each of those relationships, no matter how positive, always has its moment of real anxiety—what relationship doesn't? And all of Gaiman's selves are split, if not deliriously shattered. What he has to say about those relationships is what makes him an artist particularly interesting to our time. The Game of You is, after all, not the Game of I. (That's the "me-first" game—most of us know it only too well—where what I want is wholly above all other considerations and has to be pursued at any cost to anyone else.) It seems to me what Gaiman is saying, with the help of the artists who draw the pictures, is that, in the rich, complex, and socially constructed world around us, you cannot ultimately be what—or who—you want to be without some support from me. Wanda supports Barbie at the beginning of the story. At the end of the story, even though posthumously, Barbie supports Wanda. The element of death, however, makes it a much darker tale than that simple and rather Pollyanna reduction presupposes.

We're not talking simple altruism, here. We're talking about something much deeper, that allows individuals to exist; we're talking about the hidden, shifting, undersea reefs on which every individual stands—rocks that so rarely show clear above the tides of illusion and desire. That's the support we mean, and it always begins in something outside the self.

Gaiman is also saying that, because of death—even a fantasy death that allows articulation and information to come from beyond its borders, when magicked up by a centuries-old moon witch—no one can win the Game of I. Wanda cannot win it. Barbie cannot win it. (Morpheus tells Thessaly that, for all her longevity, she cannot win it either: take a look at the various "immortals'" deaths in Gaiman's more recent SANDMAN series, "Brief Lives...") Nor will I. Nor will you. (Also take a look at Gaiman's moving meditation on the last days of an artist, in his powerful work with Dave McKean, **Signal to Noise.**) Thus, for Gaiman, **A Game of You** is the only game worth playing—because it is the only game where, in the end, there's any chance of coming out ahead.

Even if one wins only by a name written on a stone that will wash away with the next shower, at least that allows something to persist in memory—and thus may lead to something else. But without even the name preserved momentarily in the real world by real action (and here, as I hope we can see, "real" is not the catch-all antonym for fantasy but rather a specific synonym for the political—as it is whenever it's used intelligently), there's no hope at all. Gaiman shows us the most marginal win possible in **A Game of You.**

But it's still won by moments, however small, of real social bravery. And that's what, at the end of **A Game of You,** Gaiman portrays. Thus, in a fantasy world whose tragedies are not real (i.e., not political) but are, nevertheless through that fantasy, deeply recognizable (and readable in any number of real ways), he has

a game of you

chapter one

THE LAND.

"What will we do, Prinado? Why, we will perish. We will all die, and the Land will die, and the world will die, and the Cuchoo will reign in bleak dominion over all."

"That is what we will do."

"It mus' not happen, Luz."

"Must not? With the Princess gone, what else can we do?"

"But Tantoblin. 'e swore to come. 'e swore to bring us tidings."

"The Tantoblin will not come. I felt him die. The Black Guard found him in the night."

"You're makin' it up, Luz. Imaginin' things. Honest."

"No. I felt it inside of my heart. I felt him die."

"But what tidings could the Tantoblin have brought us, save that She has abandoned us, and the Children of the Cuckoo continue to spread across the land?"

"Well, there's Colonel Knowledge. 'e once said 'e would aid our struggle..."

"He waits on the border. Perhaps he will help us. Perhaps not."

"I'm hungry."

"We're all hungry, Wilkinson."

"I never said we weren't. Did I say we weren't? I don't think anybody here heard me say we weren't. I was just pointin' out that I'm bloody starving, that's all.

"And I'm not just hungry.

"I'm hungry and I'm cold."

"Actually, I'm hungry and I'm cold, and I'm miserable and we're all going to die."

"For the love of Murphy, Wilkinson, will you stop saying that?"

"Luz said it first. I was just agreein' with her. And I am hungry."

"Martin Tenbones. You have not yet spoken. What say you?"

"I say that She has not abandoned us. And I have the Porpentine. The hierogram remains unbroken. The Land is far from lost."

"I think she mus' be dead. Or she 'as forgotten us."

"She cannot have forgotten us. But she may be hurt, in her other world. My friends, I have been thinking on this for a long time now..."

"And?"

"And it seems to me that if she cannot come to us, one of us must go to her. We must call her back."

"How?"

"I have the Porpentine. It will find her."

"But..."

"I must find her, in whatever distant world she waits. Else the land must be lost to the cold and the dark, and the Cuckoo prevail over all."

SLAUGHTER ON FIFTH AVENUE

1

WRITTEN BY *NEIL GAIMAN*
DRAWN BY *SHAWN McMANUS*
COLORED BY *DANIEL VOZZO*
LETTERED BY *TODD KLEIN*
EDITED BY *KAREN BERGER*
ASSISTED BY *ALISA KWITNEY*

SANDMAN

FEATURING CHARACTERS CREATED BY GAIMAN, KIETH AND DRINGENBERG.

BZZZZZZZZZZZZ

YEAH? I'M COMING...

BARBIE? IT'S ME, HONEY. I THOUGHT WE COULD GO SHOPPING.

WANDA? I WAS ASLEEP. COME IN.

I'M SORRY. OBVIOUSLY I'VE WRENCHED YOU OUT OF A *DELIGHTFUL* DREAM.

WHAT *WAS* IT? WRITHING ON A BEAR-SKIN WITH SOME HUNK? OR JUST ONE OF THE *DULL* ONES, WHERE YOU'RE BACK AT SCHOOL AND YOU FORGOT YOUR HOMEWORK...

I *DON'T* DREAM, WANDA.

OHHH COME ONNN, BARBIE-BOOBIE. EVERYBODY DREAMS.

I DON'T.

WELL?

WELL WHAT?

ARE WE GOING SHOPPING?

I'M BROKE.

SO'S YOUR AUNTIE WANDA. BUT DO YOU THINK I'M GOING TO LET A LITTLE THING LIKE *THAT* STOP ME?

I LOOK A MESS.

YOU'RE TALKING. WITH *THOSE* CHEEKBONES? I'D *KILL* FOR THOSE CHEEKBONES. MM. WELL, *MAIM*, MAYBE.

YOU GOT BETTER CHEEKBONES THAN ME, WANDA. GIVE ME A COUPLA MINUTES TO PUT MY FACE ON, AND WAKE UP.

YOU WANNA MAKE SOME COFFEE?

MAKE COFFEE? YOU WANT ME TO MAKE *YOU* COFFEE?

YEAH. IS THAT BENEATH YOU OR SOMETHING?

NO. IT'S JUST MY COFFEE *ALWAYS* TASTES KIND OF LIKE SOMETHING THAT'S BEEN *DEAD* FOR A WHILE.

I MAKE A *GREAT* CHOCOLATE SOUFFLÉ, THOUGH. WOULD YOU LIKE A CHOCOLATE SOUFFLÉ?

COFFEE.

OKAY. YOU DON'T KNOW *WHAT* YOU'RE MISSING.

DO YOU TAKE CREAM?

UH HUH.

SO WHERE *IS* IT?

IN THE REFRIGERATOR.

FIRST PLACE I LOOKED.

THERE'S ONLY THIS CARTON OF FUZZY *GREEN* STUFF IN THERE NOT EVEN *YOU* COULD DRINK. YOU *MIGHT* WANT TO DONATE IT TO SCIENCE, OR TAKE IT TO YOUR LEADER, BUT...

SO GO GET SOME. THE SSALY'LL HAVE CREAM. OR THE GUYS UPSTAIRS.

OH. HI, WANDA.

THESSALY? IT'S ME, WANDA. YOU IN?

YEAH. YOU GOT ANY CREAM?

I GOT SOME *SOY-MILK* STUFF. THAT OKAY?

NO. NO, I DON'T THINK SO.

IT'S FOR BARBIE.

I DON'T THINK SHE'D BE SATISFIED WITH *ANYTHING* THAT WASN'T SQUIRTED FROM THE UDDER OF A *REAL COW*.

NO. NO. SORRY.

NO PROBLEM. SEEYA, SWEET THING.

HI. HAZEL? FOXGLOVE? IT'S ME.

C'MON. OPEN UP. I *KNOW* YOU'RE IN THERE.

WE'RE NOT HERE. WE WENT OUT AGES AGO.

DON'T. THE EAGLE EYES OF SHERLOCK WANDA *CANNOT* BE FOOLED.

I'VE ALREADY SPOTTED A NUMBER OF *CLUES.* CIGARETTE ASH. PARSLEY IN THE BUTTER. ALL *THAT* SHIT.

LET ME *IN* OR I CALL OUT THE *BLOODHOUNDS.*

THANK YOU, LADIES. THIS ACT OF KINDNESS HAS TOUCHED ME MORE DEEPLY THAN YOU CAN EVER KNOW.

YOU'RE *SO FULL* OF IT, WANDA.

HI GEORGE. HOW'S IT HANGING?

WHY *I'M* JUST *DANDY.* THANK YOU *SO* MUCH FOR ASKING.

THIS? OH, DON'T WORRY. IT'S NOT *MY* CUTE FROG MUG. I'M CARRYING IT FOR A FRIEND.

OUR COFFEE, MADAME. AND WHAT ARE *WE* TODAY, THEN?

I'M A CHESS BOARD. *YOU'RE* JUST TACKY, WANDA.

OKAY. I'M READY. WHERE ARE WE GOING?

TIFFANY'S.

TIFFANY'S? YOU'RE CRAZY.

WE'RE *BROKE*, RIGHT?

YEAH.

SO IT DOESN'T MATTER *WHERE* WE GO, WE CAN'T AFFORD IT.

RIGHT.

SO WE'RE GOING TO TIFFANY'S.

OKAY.

YECCHY COFFEE.

I *WARNED* YOU.

CUTE MUG, THOUGH.

PRINCESS BARBARA? THE SUBWAY AWAITS YOU. SHAKE YOUR LITTLE BUNS...

"DON'T YOU JUST *LOVE* THE SUBWAY? I JUST HAVE TO SET FOOT ON A SUBWAY TRAIN, AND IT'S LIKE A *MAGIC CARPET.* Y'KNOW? IT COULD TAKE YOU *ANYWHERE.*"

"YEAH, THAT'S WHAT I'M AFRAID OF."

YUHGODDANYSPARECHANGE?

I GAVE AT THE OFFICE ALREADY. BUG OFF AND DIE.

HERE.

YEAHTHANKS.

EEEH. TAKE IT AWAY. I DON'T LIKE DOGS.

I DON'T LIKE DOGS. I'M SCARED OF DOGS.

I DON'T LIKE DOGS.

HEY, DON'T WORRY ABOUT *ROWLEY.* HE WON'T HURT YOU. HE'S JUST A LITTLE *PUPPY,* AREN'T YOU, ROWLEY?

I DON'T LIKE DOGS. I'M SCARED OF DOGS. I DON'T LIKE THEM.

LISTEN, HE'S A *PUPPY*, HE'S ON A *LEASH*. SO LAY OFF, WILLYA?

I'M SCARED OF DOGS. I DON'T LIKE DOGS.

I JUS' DON'T LIKE DOGS.

ANOTHER OF THE WONDERFUL SIGHTS OF OUR FAIR CITY.

DON'T.

POOR THING.

YOU GOTTA DEVELOP A THICKER HIDE IF YOU'RE GOING TO BE A REAL NEW YORKER, BARBIE-BUBULLAH.

"THIS IS A *CITY* OF *CRAZIES*. THE ART LIES IN NOT LETTING *THEM* GET TO *YOU*."

I DON'T LIKE DOGS.

"I MEAN, *JESUS*, BABY. IF I LET IT GET TO ME, I'D NEVER GO OUTSIDE THE DOOR."

"THIS *IS* THE TWILIGHT ZONE. I'M IN IT, *YOU'RE* IN IT, THE *I-DON'T-LIKE-DOGS* LADY'S IN IT. SHIT HAPPENS. THIS IS NEW YORK. 'WE CONTROL THE VERTICAL'...

DOGS. THEY SCARE ME. I'M FRIGHTENED OF 'EM.

"OR WAS THAT *THE OUTER LIMITS?*"

"SHUT UP, WANDA. IT'S *NOT* FUNNY. POOR THING. SHE WAS REALLY SCARED."

I DON'T LIKE DOGS.

BREAKFAST AT TIFFANY'S, THEN?

NOT YET. BREAKFAST FIRST. WINDOW SHOPPING LATER. OKAY?

I WANT A REAL CUP OF COFFEE. ONE I CAN DRINK.

YOU DON'T REMEMBER YOUR DREAMS, THEN?

I DON'T DREAM.

UH-UH. EVERYBODY DREAMS. I READ ABOUT IT. YOU DON'T DREAM, YOU GO KOO-KOO. NO, YOU JUST DON'T REMEMBER THEM, IS ALL.

I REMEMBER MY DREAMS.

I THOUGHT YOU SAID YOU DIDN'T--

I USED TO DREAM. I USED TO DREAM ABOUT LOTS OF THINGS.

I'D HAVE THIS WEIRD DREAM, NIGHT AFTER NIGHT. SAME DREAM-- WELL, NOT THE SAME DREAM. IT CONTINUED, Y'KNOW. LIKE A BOOK. OR A TV SHOW.

SAME TIME, SAME CHANNEL. I JUST HAD TO CLOSE MY EYES...

SO WHAT HAPPENED?

I...

I DON'T KNOW. I MEAN, IT'S ALL SORT OF MIXED TOGETHER. THAT WAS WHEN I SPLIT WITH KEN. I WENT THROUGH A LOAD OF BAD STUFF BACK THEN, AND, I DON'T KNOW...

SOMEWHERE IN ALL THAT, THE DREAMS WENT AWAY.

I DREAM. I HAVE TERRIFIC DREAMS.

NEVER ABOUT SEX, THOUGH. NOT SINCE I WAS TWELVE AND HAVING MY FIRST WET DREAMS. NOW, THEY WERE REALLY MONDO WEIRD.

I ONCE DREAMED I WAS MAKING OUT WITH WEIRDZO LILA LAKE. YOU REMEMBER THE WEIRDZOS?

WANDA, WHAT ARE YOU TALKING ABOUT?

THE WEIRDZOS, FROM THE OLD HYPERMAN COMICS. THEY LIVED ON THIS SQUARE PLANET SOMEWHERE OUT IN OUTER SPACE, AND THEY DID EVERYTHING BACKWARDS. "US DO OPPOSITE OF EARTH THINGS IN WEIRDZO WORLD."

THEY HAD THESE *WHITE* FACES, LIKE THEY WERE MADE OF CRYSTAL OR SOMETHING, AND, LIKE, THEY WERE *ALL* HYPERMAN OR HIS FRIENDS.

AND *ALL* THE WOMEN WERE LILA LAKE. THEY HAD THIS *WEIRDZO* CODE, AND--

ARE YOU OKAY?

NO. I DON'T THINK SO. I'M FEELING KIND OF WOOZY.

SO EAT. DRINK. C'MON. YOU GOTTA TAKE *CARE* OF YOURSELF.

I'M OKAY. I'LL BE FINE.

SO ARE YOU TELLING ME THAT YOU HAVEN'T DREAMED IN, WHAT, *TWO YEARS?*

YEAH, I SUPPOSE

I MEAN, I STILL REMEMBER MY *OLD DREAMS.* THERE WAS THIS BIG DOG-THING WHO WAS MY BEST FRIEND, CALLED...OHH... MISTER BONEY, OR SOMETHING LIKE THAT.

AND THE WHOLE LAND WAS IN TERRIBLE DANGER.

AND *THEN* MY LIFE KIND OF FELL APART.

IT WASN'T *KEN'S* FAULT, THOUGH. NOT *REALLY.* THERE WAS THIS ONE WEIRD NIGHT, AND AFTER THAT I WOULDN'T TALK TO HIM. I WOULDN'T... YOU KNOW. ESS EEE EX.

HE JUST WENT OFF AND FOUND SINDY.

I MEAN, WE WERE STILL *LIVING* TOGETHER, BUT HE WAS BRINGING HER *HOME.* IT GOT *REALLY* SHITTY.

HAL--HE WAS MY LANDLORD IN FLORIDA--HE'S AN OLD FRIEND OF SCARLETT'S, THEY WERE IN SOME SHOWS TOGETHER, YEARS BACK. SO HE GOT IN TOUCH WITH SCARLETT, AND SHE GOT ME THE ROOM UP HERE.

I *WANTED* TO BE A WEIRDZO, WHEN I GREW UP. WEIRDZO ALVIN.

ALVIN? THAT'S YOUR *REAL* NAME?

WANDA'S MY REAL NAME, BARBIE-BABY. *ALVIN'S* JUST THE NAME I WAS *BORN* WITH.

YOU EVER *TELL* ANYONE, BARBS, YOU'RE DEAD MEAT.

This is a bright place, filled with frightened people, and fast hard things that hurt and wound.

No matter.

I swore I would remain by her side forever, and until death divided us. I must walk until once more we are reunited.

This place is frightening, but I am not afraid.

People shout.

High stone cliffs tower upon each side of me.

I am brave. I am not afraid.

That the land may not die, I must walk this distant land, and be not afraid.

My death hovers near me, screeching and fluttering and giggling: a ghost death, in a ghost world. I tell myself I feel only ghost pain, and I will not let it hurt me.

I am not afraid.

O Princess Barbara, protect me now as I have protected you in days long past. O Murphy watch over me.

I will not be afraid.

I WASN'T ALLOWED TO READ COMICS WHEN I WAS A GIRL. POP SAID THEY WERE UNLADYLIKE.

HE USED TO SAY THAT LOTS OF THINGS WERE UNLADY-LIKE.

I WAS HIS LITTLE LADY. I WONDER WHAT HE'D SAY IF HE COULD SEE ME NOW.

SOMETIMES I LOOK IN THE MIRROR AND I DON'T RECOGNIZE ME.

I THINK MY PARENTS TELL THEIR FRIENDS I'M DEAD.

MY AUNT DORA WHO STILL TALKS TO ME--

--I MEAN SHE PRAYS FOR ME TO REPENT MY WICKED WAYS, BUT SHE TALKS AT LEAST--

--SHE SAYS THEY'VE STILL GOT MY OLD ROOM AT HOME ON THE FARM, JUST LIKE IT WAS WHEN I LEFT.

ALL MY OLD TOYS AND EVERYTHING LAID OUT ON THE BED. JUST LIKE IT'S A SHRINE OR SOMETHING.

TOYS...?

WANDA? WHAT'S HAPPENING HERE?

SORRY, FOLKS. THIS ROAD'S CLOSED. THERE'S NOTHIN' TO SEE. YOU BETTER FIND AN ALTERNATE ROUTE. I REPEAT, THERE'S NOTHIN' TO SEE...

MOVE ON...

MARTIN?

MARTIN TENBONES?

Princess?

My princess?

FIRE!

HEY! LADY! BACK OFF! THE THING MAY STILL BE *DANGEROUS*.

NO.

MARTIN TENBONES?

My princess? I came for you...

BUT YOU'RE FROM MY *DREAM*...

Princess... The Land needs you. Please, come back to us...

Fulfill your quest...

Around my neck... the Porpentine... take it...

Please, Princess. Take it.

...The Cuckoo... it will destroy us all...

THE PORPENTINE? BUT...

I love you, Princess. And I am sorry...

I said I would not leave your side, not while I lived... not... ever...

I...

OUT OF THE WAY, BIMBO.

WHAT THE HELL WAS IT?

I DUNNO, SOME KIND OF *WOLF*, MAYBE? WHO *CARES*? LOOK AT THOSE *TEETH*...

BARBIE? ARE YOU OKAY?

WHAT'S THAT YOU'VE GOT? WHAT HAPPENED?

BARBIE?

BARBIE? YOU'RE CRYING.

YEAH, IT'S DEAD.

COME ON-- WE'RE NEARLY HOME. JUST *ONE* MORE STEP. THAT'S IT. AND *ONE* MORE...

COME ON, BARBIE. KEEP WALKING FOR AUNTIE WANDA. COME ON. *ONE* MORE STEP...

THERE WE GO...NOW... JUST A *FEW* MORE TINY STEPS AND YOU'RE SNUG IN YOUR *OWN* LITTLE DEN AGAIN...

COME ON, BARBIE. *EVERYTHING'S* OKAY...

LISTEN--IF YOU WANT I CAN STAY. OR I CAN CALL SOMEONE.

AND IT WAS ONLY A *DOG,* OR SOMETHING. IT DIDN'T EVEN *HURT* YOU, BARB. I MEAN, THEY *SHOT* IT BEFORE IT COULD DO ANY *DAMAGE...*

I THINK I WANT TO BE ON MY OWN NOW.

PLEASE.

THAT'S FINE, THEN. NO PROBLEM.

I'LL JUST BE NEXT DOOR. BANG ON THE WALL IF YOU WANT ME. HAHHAHAH. YOU KNOW THE ROUTINE.

WELL, YOU, UH, GET SOME REST.

WHEW!

UH EXCUSE ME...

UH...THE UH LADY IN UH APARTMENT ONE. SHE'S UH NOT VERY WELL?

BUTT *OUT,* GEORGE. IT'S NONE OF YOUR BUSINESS. SHE'S JUST HAD A HARD DAY.

THE PORPENTINE? BUT THAT WAS ONLY IN MY DREAM...

IT'S ALL COMING BACK... MARTIN TENBONES... AND THE PORPENTINE... AND THE LAND...

AND THE SCARY THING...

THE CUCKOO.

NO.

PLEASE NO. IT ISN'T REAL...

IT WAS ONLY A DREAM.

WHAT'S HAPPENING TO ME?

YOU DON'T KNOW US, PRINCESS BARBARA.

BUT THE CHILDREN OF THE CUCKOO KNOW YOU. OH YES...

WE KNOW ALL ABOUT YOU.

End of Chapter One

game of you

chapter two

BZZZZZZ

HOLD ON!

HI, BARBIE. IT'S ME.

IS IT ALL RIGHT IF...

I MEAN...

CAN I COME IN? AND TALK? TO YOU?

SURE, HAZEL. COME IN.

I HOPE IT'S NOT TOO *LATE* OR ANYTHING. I MEAN, IF YOU WERE TRYING TO GET SOME SLEEP, I CAN GO *AWAY* AGAIN.

NO... I WASN'T TRYING TO SLEEP. YOU WANT ANY—THING?

JUST TO TALK.

I FIGURED THERE'S STUFF YOU *KNOW* THAT NO ONE ELSE HERE WOULD. I MEAN, I'M NOT SURE I CAN TALK TO FOXGLOVE ABOUT IT, AND WANDA DOESN'T KNOW FROM SHIT ABOUT THAT STUFF, AND THESSALY, I MEAN, SHE'S SO *VANILLA,* AND SCARLETT'S OUT OF TOWN, SO THAT LEFT *YOU.*

OKAY. SO WHAT DO YOU WANT TO TALK ABOUT?

HAZEL? WHAT'S THE MATTER?

WHAT DO YOU DO IF YOU THINK YOU'RE PREGNANT?

WHAT?

LOOK, IT'S A SIMPLE QUESTION AND IF YOU DON'T KNOW THE ANSWER JUST TELL ME YOU DON'T KNOW AND I'LL GO AWAY AGAIN.

HAZEL. YOU'RE. I MEAN. YOU'RE A *DYKE*.

OH *GREAT*. TELL ME SOMETHING I *DON'T* KNOW.

AND YOU *REALLY* THINK YOU MIGHT BE *PREGNANT*?

MM-HMM.

YOU WANT TO TELL ME ABOUT IT?

WELL, ABOUT SIX WEEKS BACK I WOUND UP WORKING REALLY LATE, AND ONE OF THE WAITERS GAVE ME A LIFT HOME, AND WE WERE, LIKE, BOTH A BIT DRUNK...

WELL, *FOX* HAD GONE BACK TO VISIT HER FOLKS, AND *HE* WAS SORT OF TIRED, AND HE ASKED IF HE COULD STAY OVER, SO *I* SAID *SURE*.

YOU SAID...?

WELL, HE WAS *TIRED*, SO WHAT *ELSE* WAS I GOING TO DO?

AND HE *PROMISED* NOTHING WAS GOING TO HAPPEN. AND *THEN*, WE WERE LYING TOGETHER, AND HIS THING WENT ALL HARD, AND WE SORT OF *DID* IT.

WELL, I FIGURED THERE WAS *NO WAY* I COULD GET *PREGNANT*.

YOU MEAN HE USED A *CONDOM*?

NO. BUT WE DID IT STANDING UP.

STANDING *UP*?

YEAH. SO IT *SHOULD* HAVE BEEN *FINE*.

AND IT WAS ALL OVER *REALLY* FAST. I MEAN, IT WAS KIND OF *DUMB*, BUT HE SEEMED SO SAD AND SORT OF LONELY, AND ANYWAY HE'S GAY. MOSTLY.

WELL, MY PERIODS ARE *USUALLY* PRETTY CLOCKWORK. I MEAN, ME AND FOX *ALWAYS* COME ON WITHIN A DAY OF EACH OTHER. BUT THIS TIME IT JUST DIDN'T COME...

UH...HAZEL... THIS WAITER...

RAPHAEL.

RIGHT. RAPHAEL. I MEAN, WHAT DID YOU *THINK?* WHEN HE ASKED TO STAY OVER?

I THOUGHT HE WAS REAL TIRED.

...DID YOU ENJOY IT?

NOT MUCH. IT HURT A BIT. I *CAN'T* BE PREGNANT, *CAN* I?

HAZEL... LOOK, WAS THIS YOUR *FIRST* TIME? WITH A *GUY?*

MM-HM.

OKAY. WELL, THERE ARE *KITS* YOU CAN BUY, TO CHECK IF YOU'RE PREGNANT.

I DON'T HAVE TO KILL A RABBIT, DO I?

WHAT?

I THOUGHT SOMEONE SAID AT SCHOOL THAT THE TEST WAS LIKE, IF THIS RABBIT DIED OR NOT. AND I *WON'T* KILL A RABBIT.

I'M A *VEGETARIAN.*

I *THINK* THAT WAS IN THE OLDEN DAYS. THESE DAYS IT'S JUST A BLUE RING IN YOUR PEE.

HAVE *YOU* EVER BEEN PREGNANT?

MM. ONCE.

WHAT HAPPENED?

I HAD AN ABORTION. I WAS STILL IN HIGH SCHOOL.

DOES IT *HURT?*

NOT REALLY. YOU GET AN ANAESTHETIC.

SO WHAT DO I DO?

YOU GET A HOME PREGNANCY TEST. YOU GO SEE YOUR DOCTOR. THEN YOU TALK TO FOXGLOVE AND FIGURE OUT WHAT YOU'RE GOING TO DO NEXT.

AND, LISTEN, HAZEL. WHEN IT COMES TO SEX... WELL, DON'T EVER BELIEVE ANYTHING A GUY SAYS.

GUYS THINK WITH THEIR DICKS.

OH. I MEAN, I'D HEARD PEOPLE SAY THAT. OTHER WOMEN. DYKES. BUT I FIGURED THAT WAS JUST BECAUSE THEY DIDN'T LIKE MEN...

BUT YOU LIKE MEN.

I SUPPOSE. I HAVEN'T SLEPT WITH ONE FOR TWO YEARS...

YEAH. I LIKE MEN. BUT I STILL WOULDN'T LET ONE STAY THE NIGHT UNLESS I WAS PLANNING TO SLEEP WITH HIM.

MM. CAN I HAVE THE FROG MUG? THAT WAS WHY I TOLD FOXGLOVE I WAS COMING DOWN HERE. TO GET OUR MUG BACK.

THANKS. I MEAN FOR EVERYTHING. FOR LISTENING. FOR THE ADVICE.

NO PROBLEM. LET ME KNOW HOW IT GOES. OKAY?

I WILL. SORRY.

LISTEN, YOU LOOK LIKE YOU NEED SOME SLEEP.

MAYBE I DO. G'NIGHT.

SILLY GIRL.

SHE'S *RIGHT*. I AM TIRED. BUT I'M SCARED...

I DON'T EVEN KNOW WHAT I'M SCARED OF. SOMETHING IN A DREAM I DREAMED TOO LONG AGO.

I *DON'T* WANT TO SLEEP...

TV. I'LL WATCH A LITTLE TV. THEN MAYBE I'LL GO FOR A *WALK*. WALK DOWN TO THE WATERFRONT AND STARE AT LADY LIBERTY WHILE THE SUN COMES UP...

...AND GET MUGGED AND RAPED BY A NEW YORK CRAZY BEFORE I GET *FIVE BLOCKS*. MAYBE *NOT* A GREAT IDEA.

...OF THE NEW YORK POLICE DEPARTMENT MAINTAINS THE GIANT DOG SHOT DEAD ON 5th AVENUE THIS MORNING MUST HAVE ESCAPED FROM A PRIVATE COLLECTION...

OH GOD. MARTIN TENBONES. *POOR* MARTIN TENBONES...

...OLD-FASHIONED COTTON WOOL WHEN YOU COULD BE USING *NEW WUNDAWOOL?*

NOW IN *CINNAMON, FRESHMINT,* AND *NEW SALSA* FLAVORS...

...HURRICANE LISA SHOULD BLOW ITSELF OUT HARMLESSLY OVER THE NORTH ATLANTIC...

SHE'S SUCH A *BEAUTIFUL BABY*, BARBIE. WE THINK WE'LL NAME HER AFTER *YOU*.

AND SHE'LL BE AVAILABLE IN CINNAMON, FRESHMINT, OR NEW SALSA FLAVOR.

THESSALY'S VANILLA.

MIDNIGHT.

GEORGE WAITS, PATIENTLY.

FOXGLOVE CHEERFULLY ROLLED OVER WHEN HER ADVANCES WERE REBUFFED, AND IS ALREADY SNORING GENTLY.

HAZEL IS READING HERSELF TO SLEEP WITH RAYMOND CHANDLER'S *THE LONG GOODBYE.*

EACH NIGHT, BEFORE BED, THESSALY BRUSHES HER HAIR ONE HUNDRED TIMES.

SHE COUNTS EACH BRUSH STROKE.

WANDA SURFACES TO THE LOW BUZZ OF TELEVISION VOICES IN THE NEXT APARTMENT.

BARBIE, SHE THINKS. *THIN GODDAMN WALLS,* SHE THINKS.

AND THEN THE WARM DARKNESS TAKES HER BACK...

AND BARBIE?

BARBIE DREAMS.

LULLABIES OF BROADWAY
2

NEIL GAIMAN : WRITER
SHAWN McMANUS: ARTIST
DANIEL VOZZO : COLORIST
TODD KLEIN : LETTERER
ALISA KWITNEY: ASST. ED.
KAREN BERGER : EDITOR

THE
SANDMAN

SANDMAN CHARACTERS CREATED BY NEIL GAIMAN, SAM KIETH AND MIKE DRINGENBERG

ONE O'CLOCK.

ALL ASLEEP.

THEY'RE ALL ASLEEP.

ALL ASLEEP THEY'RE ALL ASLEEP, EVERYBODY IS ALL ASLEEP...

MEN'S ASLEEP, LADIES ASLEEP, EVERY-BODIES IS ALL ASLEEP...

EVERYBODY BUT ME'S ASLEEP...

EVERYBODY BUT US.

WANDA DREAMS.

DO YOU HAVE ANY NICE DRESSES?

WE HAVE LOTS OF NICE DRESSES. I WILL GIVE YOU ALL THE NICE DRESSES YOU WANT.

WILL I HAVE TO PAY FOR THEM?

YOU WILL NOT HAVE TO PAY FOR THEM.

1/2 OF

WE WERE AT SCHOOL WITH YOU, WANDA.

WE ARE SO ENVIOUS.

BECAUSE I DO NOT BEAR A GRUDGE, I WILL GIVE ALL OF YOU NICE DRESSES AS WELL.

HURRAH!

ALVIN? IT AM ME, WEIRDZO LILA.

WEIRDZO LILA NO. 1

MY NAME ISN'T ALVIN. IT'S WANDA.

I'M A WOMAN.

SAL

YOU AM? THAT AM WONDERFUL NEWS! US MUST TELL WEIRDZO NUMBER ONE!

YES! THAT AM *TERRIBLE* NEWS! ME AM *SO* HAPPY!

US MUST OPERATE *IMMEDIATELY* TO MAKE YOU *IMPERFECT.*

DOCTORS! NURSES!

WEIRDZO NO. 1

NO-- PLEASE.

I'M *SCARED* OF SURGERY. I CAN'T DO IT. I CAN'T GO THROUGH WITH IT. PLEASE...

INNOCENCE AM *NO* EXCUSE. HIM WILL *THANK* US ONE DAY. HIM WILL SAY, "WEIRDZO, YOU FINK. YOU CUT IT OFF. GET LOST."

OKAY. MAKE HIM READY FOR SURGERY.

FOR *GOD'S* SAKE! YOU CAN'T *DO* THIS TO ME. I'M *SCARED* OF SURGERY. I WON'T DO IT. I *WON'T* DO IT...

LISTEN. HIM BE SO HAPPY US GOING TO OPERATE ON HIM.

IT AM SO GOOD. MAYBE HIM GIVE US PRESENTS AFTER.

SO WHAT YOU AM? A MAN OR A WOMAN?

WHATEVER YOU AM, WE MAKE IT BETTER.

NO.

...MMF... NO...JRM...

HAZEL DREAMS.

I'm on a train journey across a country I don't know. I don't know if I speak the language or not.

I don't know if I have a ticket.

A ticket inspector tells me that there is something wrong with my ticket. I have to go with him.

I didn't know that there were steps on trains.

He tells me there are cellars under all trains in this country. I have to go down.

The present I won with my ticket is in the box. I go to open it.

The baby smells of formaldehyde, not unpleasantly. It is cold and slightly clammy to the touch.

The autopsy scar is sewn together with black silk thread. It has been dead exactly seventy years.

It is perfectly preserved.

Foxglove is waiting for me, with her baby.

I cannot remember her baby's name. I cannot remember how old it is.

It's a boy, though. I remember that.

My baby is cold, so we put them together in a crib, to warm it up.

We love our babies.

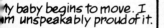

My baby begins to move. I am unspeakably proud of it.

Now it smells of roses.

NO...

I know what it's going to do. I want to hide. I want to turn away. I want to stop looking.

I can't.

I hear Fox keening for her son. I cannot move.

And I know: once it's finished with Fox's child...

(Stop it, says Fox. Stoppit stoppitstoppitstoppit...)

Then it will come for us...

DONNA?

DONNA
CAVANAGH?

GO AWAY.
LEAVE ME
ALONE.

DONNA.

IT'S FOXGLOVE,
NOW. THAT'S WHAT
I'M CALLED. I
HAVEN'T BEEN
DONNA FOR TWO
YEARS. MORE
MAYBE.

DONNA'S SOMEBODY
ELSE. DONNA'S DEAD.

DONNA.

DON'T CALL
ME THAT! WHO'S
TALKING, ANYWAY?
WHO IS THAT?

IT'S ME.
JUDY.

JUDY?
YOU
CAN'T BE
JUDY. YOU'RE
DEAD.

YEAH. DEAD
AS A DODO. IT'S
A REAL SHIT,
ISN'T IT?

AND IT'S YOUR FAULT.
YOU KNOW THAT?

MINE...?

SURE IT IS. IF
YOU HADN'T TAKEN
OFF, I WOULDN'T
HAVE BEEN HANGING
AROUND IN THAT
DAMNED DINER...

AND I'D STILL BE
ABLE TO TASTE, AND
FEEL, AND DREAM...

SO, YOU *WITH* ANYONE THESE DAYS?

...YES.

YEAH? WHAT'S HER *NAME?*

HAZEL.

IS SHE AS *PRETTY* AS ME? *IS* SHE?

DOES *SHE* MAKE YOU FEEL LIKE *I* MADE YOU FEEL?

NO...

NO SHE'S *NOT.* BUT SHE'S *NEVER* HIT ME.

ARE YOU A *GHOST?*

SOMETHING LIKE THAT. A GHOST, OR A DREAM. I DON'T KNOW. DOES IT MATTER?

DONNA...

I JUST WANT US TO BE TOGETHER AGAIN. FOR *ALWAYS.*

I WANT IT TO BE *JUST* LIKE IT *WAS.*

HOLD ON.

I GOT SOMETHING IN MY EYE...

THESSALY SLEEPS.

HMM.

NASTY LITTLE THING, AREN'T YOU?

HMM.

=KNOCK
KNOCK=

UH, WHO
IS IT?

HELLO?

HELLO? IT'S *GEORGE*,
ISN'T IT?

I MEAN, WE'VE
SAID HI, BUT WE'VE
NEVER REALLY BEEN
INTRODUCED.

I'M
THESSALY, FROM
DOWNSTAIRS...

CAN
I COME
IN?

THE LAND:

So... D'you remember us?

Yeah. Well, I'm Wilkinson. The lady's Luz.

I DON'T *KNOW*. SORT OF. I MEAN, IT'S COMING BACK TO ME, SORT OF, *BUT...*

And the gentleman in the hat is Prinado.

THANKS, I'M BARBIE.

Princess Barbara. The heir to the land.

An' its destined savior, Luz. You mustn't forget that.

Oh yeah. Right. Great. You're going to save the land?

You're going to defeat the Black Guard, and the Cuckoo, all right. And you don't even know where you are...

Well, at least Martin Tenbones knows what he's doin'.

AN' COME TO THAT, WHERE IS THE GREAT HAIRY WOSSNAME?

I THOUGHT HE'D BE COMING BACK WITH YOU.

HE'S DEAD.

I see.

THEN WE ARE LOST.

THE CUCKOO HAS WON.

DON' SAY THAT, LUZ.

NO. SHE'S RIGHT.

WHAT GOOD AM I GOING TO BE?

SHUT UP!

For the grace of Murphy: she's the Princess, isn't she? Well, isn't she?

And she's got the Porpentine.

And the hierogram is still unbroken.

Do you think he'd've wanted us to give up now?

Well? Do you?

I... I don't know...

This place I had to get to. This "Brightly Shining Sea."

Is it a long way away?

Too far. We need to cross this mountain range; to avoid the Black Guard.

And between us and the Sea is the Citadel of the Cuckoo...

It's a very long way.

I see. Well, then...

We'd better get going.

End of Chapter Two.

a game of you

chapter three

NEW YORK. 2:00 AM.

LEAVE ME ALONE, JUDY... BY THE GODDESS... JUST LEAVE ME...

NO!

ALONE...

HAZEL? IS THAT YOU?

I... I THINK... I HAD A *BAD* DREAM...

SOME KIND OF NIGHTMARE...

SHIT!

YEAH. I WAS... I THINK I WAS HAVING A DREAM TOO. A *REALLY* BAD ONE. THERE WAS THIS... SOMEBODY I USED TO KNOW...

IT WAS LIKE IT WAS REALLY *HAPPENING*...

3 BAD MOON RISING

SANDMAN

WRITTEN BY NEIL GAIMAN • DRAWN BY COLLEEN DORAN •
COLORED BY DANIEL VOZZO • LETTERED BY TODD KLEIN •
EDITED BY KAREN BERGER • ASSISTED BY ALISA KWITNEY

FEATURING CHARACTERS CREATED
BY GAIMAN, KIETH & DRINGENBERG

YOU KNOW THE *REALLY SCARY* THING ABOUT BAD DREAMS?

THE FACT YOU THINK IT'S REALLY HAPPENING?

UH-*UH*. NOT THAT.

IT'S THAT *SOMETHING'S GOING ON IN YOUR* HEAD, AND YOU CAN'T *CONTROL* IT. I MEAN, IT'S LIKE THERE'S THESE *BAD WORLDS* INSIDE YOU. BUT IT'S JUST *YOU*...

IT'S LIKE YOU'RE BETRAYING YOURSELF.

KNOCK KNOCK!

HELLO? FOXGLOVE? HAZEL? HELLO?

IS ANYBODY *THERE?*

HELLO. IT'S *ME*. THESSALY. I THINK YOUR DOORBELL'S STOPPED WORKING.

I CAME DOWN TO SEE IF YOU TWO WERE OKAY.

SURE. WE'RE *FINE*. WHY *SHOULDN'T* WE BE FINE?

MM-HMM. WELL, THANKS FOR UM. STOPPING BY.

NO BAD DREAMS?

75

WELL, CHEER UP: THE CAVALRY ARE ON THEIR WAY INTO YOUR DREAMS, TO HELP YOU FIGHT A SCARY NUMBER CALLED THE CUCKOO WHO WANTS YOU DEAD.

UNLESS THIS IS ALL SOME PARANOID WITCHY FANTASY OF THESSALY'S. WHICH IS AS POSSIBLE AS ANYTHING ELSE.

BRR. THE SCARIEST LITTLE MISS GOODY-TWO-SHOES I EVER MET. I KEPT EXPECTING HER TO TURN INTO MARGARET HAMILTON...

BIZARRE, HUH?

BUT, JESUS, WE'RE THE GOOD GUYS--YOU AND ME AND FOXGLOVE AND HAZEL. AND THESSALY. MAYBE.

I OUGHTA GET FOX TO WRITE ONE OF HER STORIES ABOUT US.

UM... THE BIMBOS OF NIGHT.

NIGHT OF THE BIMBOS.

THE NIGHT BIMBOS...

"BIMBOS OF DER NIGHT. VOT MUSIC ZEY MAKE. HEHEHEH..."

ONLY JOKING.

RIGHT. I'M GUARDING YOU. I HOPE YOU APPRECI-ATE THAT.

IT'S JUST YOU AND ME, DULLINK. YOU, ME, AND A SKINNED CORPSE IN THE BATHTUB.

I'M NOT GOING BACK IN THERE, I'M WARNING YOU.

IF WORST COMES TO WORST, I'LL PEE OUT THE WINDOW.

IT'S GONNA BE A LONG NIGHT...

UH EXCUSE ME UH MISS WANDA.

UH CAN WE TALK?

End of Chapter Three

RATES
$1.10 FIRST 1/9 MILE
10¢ EACH ADDITIONAL 1/9 MILE

chapter four

THE LAND.

THEY'VE TOLD ME THAT THIS IS THE MOST RISKY PART OF THE JOURNEY.

RISKY. NOT DANGEROUS. RISKY.

THERE'S NO COVER ON THE PLAIN. IF THE BLACK GUARD SPOT US, THAT'S IT. NOWHERE TO GO. NOWHERE TO RUN.

IF WE MAKE IT ACROSS THE PLAIN THERE'S A FOREST. "IT'S NOT A SAFE PLACE," SAID WILKINSON. "NOT BY A LONG SHOT. BUT THERE'S PLENTY OF COVER, AND THERE'S NO LOVE LOST BETWEEN THE TREES AND THE CUCKOO.

"NOT THAT THEY'RE ON OUR SIDE, MIND YOU, ALTHOUGH MOST OF THE TREES ARE ALL RIGHT. KEEP THEMSELVES TO THEMSELVES, UNLESS THEY'RE BOTHERED, AND ONLY AN IDIOT BOTHERS A TREE."

THAT'S WHAT HE SAID.

HEY TELL ME THERE ARE BAD THINGS IN THE FOREST. 'VE BEEN TOLD TO PRAY WE DON'T MEET ANY TWEENERS. HATEVER THEY ARE...

UT IT'LL BE WARMER THERE. AND F WE'RE LUCKY, THERE'LL BE FOOD.

HAVEN'T EATEN SINCE I GOT TO THE AND, LATE LAST NIGHT. WE'RE RINKING MELTED SNOW. I'M STARVING.

'M WEARING A PRETTY PARTY DRESS-- HE KIND I ALWAYS IMAGINED RINCESSES WOULD WEAR, WHEN WAS LITTLE.

I'M COLD.

I'M SO COLD.

4: BEGINNING TO SEE THE LIGHT

Written by Neil Gaiman, drawn by Shawn McManus, lettered by Todd Klein, colored by Daniel Vozzo. Edited by Zach's Mom, Karen Berger, assisted by Alisa Kwitney.

Sandman features characters created by Neil Gaiman, Sam Kieth, and Mike Dringenberg.

COME ON. LET'S CHECK IT OUT.

SO, WILKINSON. WHAT'S ON THE OTHER SIDE OF THE FOREST?

Once past the forest, we're in trouble again.

There's people living there, really down all the way to the sea.

WHAT *KIND* OF PEOPLE?

Just normal people. Like me, or you, or Luz here.

Or me. Or Prinado.

They used to be subjects of the Heiromancer. But...

I...*REMEMBER* THE HIEROMANCER. I MET HIM, WHEN I WAS HERE BEFORE. HE WAS A *SWEET* OLD GUY. KIND OF LIKE MY GRANDFATHER. WHAT *HAPPENED* TO HIM?

He's dead. I expect that he's dead. If he's *lucky* he's dead.

Then we come to the Citadel of the Cuckoo.

Maybe we can avoid it. Maybe. But it stands between us and the Brightly Shining Sea.

If we get to the sea, there's a causeway that leads to the Isle of Thorns. That's where you've got to get to. With the Porpentine.

'Cos that's where the Hierogram is. Or so Martin Tenbones maintains.

I hope *you'll* know what to do when we get that far because none of *us* have a clue~~

SHH. LOOK!

Oh no...

OH, HOW *GHASTLY*. THE POOR *THING*.

Murphy protect us~~ it's the Cantoblin. I knew he was dead. I felt him die.

'E was carrying a message for us.

'E still 'as it.

Look.

'ere it is. Do you want to read it *now?* It may be important.

I REMEMBER HIM.

"MARTIN TENBONES AND I WERE ON OUR WAY TO THE ARCH OF THE PORPENTINE, WHEN WE WERE ATTACKED BY THESE WHITE GRUB THINGS, LIKE FAT CHILDREN.

"SOME PEOPLE HELPED US ESCAPE -- THEY WERE CARRYING THIS *ROOM* AROUND WITH THEM."

I MEAN, IT WASN'T A *BIG* ROOM, OR ANYTHING. BUT WE WENT INTO IT, AND WHEN WE CAME *OUT*, WE WERE SOMEWHERE *ELSE*. SOMEWHERE CLOSER TO WHERE WE *WANTED* TO BE.

"AND THIS *GUY* WAS WAITING FOR US, AND HE MADE US BREAKFAST. I *LIKED* HIM."

Aye, that was the Cantoblin right enough.

Then, when the Cuckoo crushed the rest of the Room Patrol, he became a courier...

... taking tidings of the resistance to different parts of the Land.

WE HAVE TO *BURY* HIM.

But the ground is harder than ice, and we only have our paws...

THEN WE'LL COVER HIM WITH *SNOW*. MAKE A *CAIRN*.

...eave it out, gal. There's more snow on its way. And every second that passes, the Cuckoo's forces come closer to findin' us~

NO. WE *BURY* HIM.

I OWE HIM THAT MUCH.

Yes, Princess.

Right. What are we waiting for? Let's bury the poor bugger.

I ONLY *MET* YOU ONCE, BUT YOU *FED* ME, AND YOU WERE *GOOD* TO ME, AND YOU *DIED* IN MY SERVICE, TANTOBLIN.

Murphy's peace be with you.

BE AT PEACE.

OKAY, LET'S GO.

Look! Shelter! let's get up in there until the worst of it's over.

I SUPPOSE THE SNOW WOULD HAVE BURIED THE TANTOBLIN ANYWAY...

PRINADO-- LET'S TAKE A LOOK AT THE *SCROLL* YOU TOOK FROM HIM. IT MAY BE IMPORTANT.

'Ere it is, Princess.

Princess? Is that a picture of you?

YES. I'VE BEEN DOING A LOT OF FACE-PAINTING RECENTLY. ORIGINALLY I WAS GOING TO GET A TATTOO. BUT I DON'T WANT ANYTHING *PERMANENT* ANYMORE.

IT'S LIKE I CAN BE A DIFFERENT PERSON EVERY DAY.

WHERE DID HE GET THE PHOTOS FROM?

THIS IS *WEIRD.* MAYBE THE SCROLL EXPLAINS WHAT THE PHOTOS ARE ABOUT...

"*THE EUROPEAN CUCKOO (CUCULUS CANORUS) WINTERS IN THE...*" HUHN? WHAT THE HELL *IS* THIS?

Read it, my Princess. The Tantoblin thought it was important. He gave his life bringing it to us.

THE EUROPEAN CUCKOO (CUCULUS CANORUS) WINTERS IN THE TROPICS, AND IS AN ABUNDANT SUMMER VISITOR TO CONTINENTAL EUROPE AND BRITAIN, ARRIVING IN EARLY APRIL.

"IT TAKES ITS NAME FROM ITS DISTINCTIVE SONG. THE CUCKOO DOES NOT ITSELF BUILD NESTS; INSTEAD IT PLACES ITS EGGS IN THE NESTS OF OTHER BIRDS.

"THE SPECIES MOST VICTIMIZED TEND TO BE THE TREE-PIPIT, PIED WAGTAIL, HEDGE SPARROW, REDBREAST AND REED-WARBLER.

"INDEED, A BIRD WILL BROOD THE FOSTER-CHICK WHILST HER OWN INFANTS LIE SLOWLY DYING OUTSIDE THE NEST.

"THOUGH SMALL BIRDS INSTINCTIVELY MOB THE CUCKOO, WHEN AN EGG IS IN THE NEST AND AFTER THE ABNORMAL FLEDGLING IS HATCHED, NO ATTEMPT IS MADE TO DISLODGE IT.

"FOR WHEN HATCHED THE YOUNG CUCKOO, DURING THE FIRST FEW DAYS OF ITS NAKED, BLIND AND APPARENTLY HELPLESS EXISTENCE, THROWS OUT THE UNHATCHED EGGS OR FELLOW NESTLINGS.

"AFTER A WHILE THE MURDEROUS INSTINCT PASSES AND ANY NESTLINGS THAT ARE TOO HEAVY TO HAVE BEEN THROWN OUT ARE ACCEPTED AS BED-MATES. AS A RULE THE YOUNG CUCKOO GETS THE NEST TO ITSELF.

"APPARENTLY THE VOICE OF THE YOUNG CUCKOO HAS A COMMANDING, ALMOST HYPNOTIC POWER..."

Shh. Quiet.

Danger.

WE SAT THERE IN SCARED SILENCE AS THEY MARCHED PAST US, ONE BY ONE, THEIR BOOTS TRAMPING QUIETLY ON THE FRESH SNOW.

THEY CAME SO CLOSE.

I COULD HAVE REACHED OUT AND TOUCHED ONE. I COULD HAVE REACHED OUT, BUT I DID NOT.

BLACK GLISTENING ARMOR. I HAD NO DOUBT THEY WERE SEARCHING FOR US, AND HAD A BRIE MAD IMPULSE TO SCREA TO RUN OUT, TO LAUGH, TO SAY, "HERE WE ARE!"

HIDE AND SEEK...

BUT I SAT THERE LISTENING TO MY BREATHING, LISTENING TO MY HEART THUMPING IN MY CHEST, POUNDING LIKE A DRUM IN ONE OF THOSE CRAPPY LATE-NIGHT JUNGLE MOVIES.

I COULD HEAR IT. AND I KNEW *THEY* WOULD TOO.

JESUS CHRIST, I COULD HAVE *TOUCHED* THEM. ALL THEY HAD TO *DO* WAS BEND DOWN AND THEY'D'VE *SEEN* US.

THIRTY OF THEM. I COUNTED. WHEN THE LAST ONE HAD MARCHED PAST OUR SHELTER, WE WAITED IN SILENCE.

NOTHING ELSE STIRRED.

SOON THE SNOW DIED DOWN, AND AN EARLY TWILIGHT FELL, AND WE RECOMMENCED OUR JOURNEY.

NOTHING ELSE BAD HAPPENED CROSSING THE PLAIN; ALTHOUGH WHEN I TRIED LOOKING AT THEM AGAIN I SAW THAT THE POLAROIDS HAD CHANGED INTO OLD PLAYING CARDS, WHILE THE WORDS ON THE SCROLL HAD RUN TOGETHER, AND WERE BLURRED AND UNREADABLE.

THAT NIGHT WE SLEPT IN A DITCH, THE FOUR OF US HUDDLED TOGETHER FOR WARMTH.

I DO NOT REMEMBER DREAMING.

THE DREAMING.

"Which of the Skerries?"

"WELL, *THIS* ONE, LORD. IT'S HERE ON THE MAP. *LOOK.* YOU SEE?"

"I See. And you are certain this is the same one?"

"I'M CERTAIN, LORD. I FOUND IT IN THE ARCHIVES. THERE CAN BE *NO* MISTAKE. I HAVE THE *COMPACT* HERE FOR YOUR INSPECTION."

Let me see it.

Hmmm.

It comes back to me now, Lucien. But it was a very long time ago. I had thought the Skerry long-since crumbled; the compact forgotten and void.

I was in error. Ah well. We must wait and see how things fall.

NH. EXCUSE ME, SIR. YOU MAY NOT REMEMBER ME. MY NAME'S NUALA. I WAS A FAERIE GIFT.

NUALA.

YES. *RIGHT.* WELL. I WAS TOLD TO WATCH THE DREAMS OF THE MORTAL WOMAN. *BARBIE.* AND NOT *DO* ANYTHING.

WELL. I...

I *DID* SOMETHING. WHEN SHE FIRST STARTED TO DREAM. I SORT OF TRIED TO *WARN* HER. THAT THERE WAS BAD STUFF GOING DOWN. I COULDN'T JUST STAND BY AND NOT *DO* ANYTHING...

I THOUGHT I SHOULD *TELL YOU. I'M SORRY.*

I see.

Thank you for telling me, Nuala.

That will be all.

Nuala? You did the right thing.

You're smilin' this morning. That's not something I expected to see in a hurry.

MMM? OH. HI, WILKINSON. I'M WARM. I CAN'T BELIEVE IT. I THOUGHT I WAS NEVER GOING TO BE WARM AGAIN. WHERE ARE WE?

The forest borders. You hungry?

OOH. I WISH YOU HADN'T ASKED. YES, I'M STARVING.

Well, Prinado's up trees lookin' for eggs, and Luz is barterin' with the Gniedrig for fire.

Here, take my hat. Only pick the white mushrooms with the pink gills.

OKAY.

Close call last night. There but for the grace of Murphy went we. Hacked into messy little chunks.

I wasn't scared, of course. Not ME. Nerves and whiskers of steel I've got.

SURE YOU HAVE.

I saw the first of 'em, this boot goin' past, black as midnight's arsehole, I thought, you're just lucky, mate.

If I wasn't lookin' after the young lady, you'd be for it.

WILKINSON?

Yes?

WHAT'S THE HIEROGRAM?

It's um. Well, it's um. It's sort of more like an um. Well...

YOU DON'T KNOW?

Martin Ten-bones did.

I suppose we'll just have to burn that bridge when we come to it.

YEAH. I WISH I KNEW WHAT I WAS GOING TO HAVE TO DO.

"Wish in one hand, shit in the other, see which fills up first."

Old Wilkinson family saying.

Which reminds me. There's a stream just down there. Do your necessaries, and wash up afterwards. The others 'll be back soon.

Then we'll have breakfast.

THAT WAS *WONDERFUL*. REALLY, GUYS. THAT WAS AN *INCREDIBLE* BREAKFAST. I DON'T THINK I'VE EVER *HAD* A BETTER MEAL... BUT...

BUT HOW COME I COULD *TASTE* IT? I DIDN'T THINK YOU COULD TASTE THINGS IN DREAMS.

This isn't a dream.

It *is* a dream.

Well, yes, it is a dream.

But not in the way she means.

Is still a dream.

Before you came, before the cuckoo, the Land was 'ere.

HUH? BUT IF IT'S *MY* DREAM...

No. You come 'ere to dream. But the Land is older than you, Princess.

HOW-- HOW DO YOU *KNOW*?

Well, just look around you. Did *you* create all this?

I DON'T KNOW. *DIDN'T* I?

No. Course you didn't. You're just the Princess.

ANYWAY-- *ALL* I'M SAYING IS I'M *REALLY* HAPPY. I CAN'T REMEMBER EVER *BEING* SO HAPPY BEFORE.

NOT WHEN I WAS FIRST DATING KEN.

NOT EVEN WHEN I WAS A LITTLE BITTY KID, HAVING PICNICS WITH MY TOYS. I'M JUST...

...HAPPY.

I loved bein' a kid. I was one of seventeen children.

We were all named Wilkinson~~ I suppose it was roughest on the girls, but we all got used to it in the end.

I blame the parents, really.

I WAS AN ONLY CHILD.

I would've liked to've bin an only child. That way when someone shouts Wilkinson, you know if it's you or not.

Mustn't grumble. Our parents were the salt of the earth.

Lovely people. It was just when they found a name they liked, they stuck with it.

I...MY CHILDHOOD WAS...FINE, I SUPPOSE. I MEAN, MY MOM AND POP WERE NICE PEOPLE, GOOD PEOPLE.

IT JUST WASN'T VERY EXCITING.

Someone's watching us.

They've bin watchin' us since we entered the forest.

But if it was the Cuckoo's people, they'd've nobbled us by now.

So what should we do now?

WE KEEP GOING. WHAT ELSE CAN WE DO?

WE WALKED THROUGH THE FOREST FOR DAYS. ALL THE TIME I FOUND MYSELF IMAGINING EYES UPON ME, PEERING FROM BEHIND TREES.

DARKNESS. THE SMELL OF LEAVES AND TWIGS. SMALL RUSTLINGS. THE FOREST IS NOT A COMFORTING PLACE FOR TRAVELLERS.

BUT WE WERE WARM, AND WE HAD JUST ABOUT ENOUGH TO EAT. SOMETIMES THAT'S ALL THAT'S IMPORTANT.

AFTER A WHILE I SIMPLY ACCEPTED THAT WE WERE BEING FOLLOWED AND OBSERVED, JUST AS I GOT USED TO A DIET OF APPLES AND NUTS, AND DRINKING FROM SMALL STREAMS AND BROOKS, AND USING MOSS FOR TOILET PAPER.

I FELT LIKE BILBO IN MIRKWOOD, IN THAT BIT WHERE THE GIANT SPIDERS GET THEM.

WILKINSON? ARE THERE--ARE THERE GIANT SPIDERS AROUND HERE?

Giant Spiders? Round here? Course not.

SORRY. SILLY OF ME.

Nah. The Giant Spiders is all in a little forest to the west of here.

They are good people. They are loyal to you, not to the Cuckoo. But they are few in number, and timid beasts.

OH.

THAT'S NICE.

WILKINSON CLAIMED, WHEN I SPOKE TO HIM, TO HAVE AN INSTINCT FOR DIRECTION.

ACTUALLY HE TOOK HIS LEAD FROM PRINADO, WHO, FROM TIME TO TIME, WOULD CLIMB EASILY INTO THE HIGH BRANCHES, AND SCOUT THE WAY AHEAD.

AS WE GOT FURTHER INTO THE FOREST THE TREES BECAME SO THICK WE LOST THE SUN COMPLETELY. THE LIGHT THAT DID FILTER THROUGH THE LEAVES WAS STAINED GREEN AND GOLD BY DAY, COOL MOONLIGHT-BLUE BY NIGHT.

AND THEN, ONE DAY, PRINADO DIDN'T COME BACK.

But what do we do? Without Prinado we are lost...

Mm. There are meant to be paths, somewhere in the forest. Really old ones, from before there was even a forest here.

Don't know how we'd find one, mind you.

WE'RE HEADING TOWARDS THE *SEA*, AREN'T WE?

Yes.

THEN SHOULDN'T WE BE LOOKING FOR *STREAMS* AND *RIVERS*? THEY'LL BE FLOWING *INTO* THE SEA, AFTER ALL.

So we follow a stream...?

That's really smart.

DO YOU ... DO YOU THINK PRINADO'S ALL RIGHT?

no.

PRINADO?

WILKINSON? LUZ?

WAKE UP!

PRINADO'S BACK. I THINK.

Prinado? Prinado old buddy?

Is that you?

No....it's not.

WHO--WHO ARE YOU?

DO YOU SERVE THE CUCKOO?

Hhhhh...We are Tweeners...

We do not serve the Cuckoo.

WE SERVE NO-ONE but ourselves. The Tweeners belong to the Tweeners, and these are our woods.

WE WERE here before the Cuckoo. We were here before you.

Tweeners?

RUN! Just run!

Cannot escape tweeners.

These are tweener woods.

Hhhh

OW!

THE *PORPENTINE!* LOOK AT IT!

WHY'VE THEY *STOPPED COMING?*

The path.

It's one of Murphy's paths. I thought they were all *lost...*

...but the Porpentine remembers.

As long as we follow the light of the Porpentine we'll be safe.

BUT THE *TWEENERS?*

They cannot walk on this path.

IN SADNESS AND FEAR WE WALKED DOWN THE RUINED PATH, GUIDED BY THE LIGHT OF THE PORPENTINE.

THERE WAS NO MORE SLEEP THAT NIGHT FOR ANY OF US.

AS THE SUN CAME UP THE LIGHT OF THE PORPENTINE FADED. BUT THE PATH WAS STILL THERE -- OLD AND BROKEN, BUT ALWAYS VISIBLE: JUST.

THE STONES OF THE PATH WERE OLD. REALLY OLD.

"FOLLOW THE YELLOW BRICK ROAD" KEPT RUNNING THROUGH MY HEAD. BUT THE STONES WERE NOT BRICKS, AND THEY WERE DIRTY GREY.

SOON WE COULD HEAR THE CRIES OF DISTANT SEAGULLS. THERE WAS SALT IN THE AIR, AND THE LOW MUTED CRASH OF BREAKERS.

AND THEN THE FOREST ENDED, AND SO DID THE PATH.

SO THAT'S THE CITY. AND THAT'S THE SEA. WELL, WHAT DO WE DO NOW?

We've got to get you through the town, and down to the Isle of Thorns.

I'll go down and fetch help.

Luz, girl, it's too dangerous.

No, Wilkinson. You must stay here. Guard the Princess.

I will seek out the resistance. They can hide her for as long as is needed.

ARE YOU SURE, Luz?

I am sure. Alone, I have a chance. Together we have none.

You stay here. I will be back by nightfall.

GOOD LUCK, LUZ. HURRY BACK.

I will, Princess. Do not worry. I will be fine.

SO UH DON'T YOU WANT TO TALK TO ME? I KNOW UH LOTS OF THINGS. WHEN YOU'RE UH DEAD THERE'S STUFF THEY DON'T BOTHER KEEPING SECRET ANY MORE.

THAT SO?

OKAY, GEORGE, WHY'D THEY LEAVE ME BEHIND TO LOOK AFTER BARBIE?

THAT'S UH PRETTY EASY. IT'S BECAUSE YOU'RE A MAN. THAT STUFF THEY DID WITH THE UH MOON. THAT WAS A WOMEN THING.

I AM NOT A MAN.

MAYBE NOT TO YOU, YOU'RE NOT. BUT YOU'VE GOT THE UH, YOU KNOW. MALE NASTY THING.

LISTEN: I'VE HAD ELECTROLYSIS. I'M TAKING HORMONES. ALL THAT'S LEFT IS JUST A LITTLE LUMP OF FLESH; BUT ALL THAT DOESN'T MATTER...

INSIDE I'M A WOMAN.

SHE DOESN'T THINK SO.

AND TO BE HONEST UH WELL EVEN IF YOU HAD UH HAD THE OPERATION IT WOULDN'T MAKE MUCH DIFFERENCE TO THE UH MOON. IT'S CHROMOSOMES AS MUCH AS UH ANYTHING.

..IT'S LIKE UH GENDER ISN'T SOMETHING YOU CAN PICK AND CHOOSE AS UH FAR AS GODS ARE CONCERNED.

WELL, THAT'S SOMETHING THE GODS CAN TAKE AND STUFF UP THEIR SACRED RECTA.

I KNOW WHAT I AM.

I'LL UH TELL YOU SOMETHING ELSE. MESSING WITH THE MOON LIKE UH SHE DID. THAT'S DANGEROUS. I MEAN REALLY DANGEROUS.

DRAWING DOWN THE UH MOON. THESSALY WASN'T JUST DOING SOMETHING UH SPIRITUAL. THAT WAS UH PHYSICAL TOO.

I UH HATE TO THINK WHAT SHE DID TO THE UH TIDES. AND THE UH WEATHER.

SHE SHOULDN'T MESS WITH THE UH MOON. THAT'S DANGEROUS.

YOU KNOW YOU *SHOULD* BE UH WORRIED. I MEAN *REALLY* WORRIED.

YEAH? *YOU* DON'T SEEM TOO WORRIED.

WHAT HAVE I GOT TO BE WORRIED ABOUT? I'M DEAD.

WHY ARE YOU *TELLING* ME THIS?

OH, YOU KNOW. IT'S UH NICE TO HAVE SOMEONE TO UH TALK TO. AND US GUYS *SHOULD* STICK TOGETHER.

I AM *NOT* A...

LISTEN, UM GEORGE. HOW COME YOU CAN TALK? I THOUGHT THESSALY TOLD YOU TO STAY QUIET.

THESSALY'S *GONE.* HER UH COMMANDS ONLY HOLD WHILE SHE'S *HERE.*

DOES THAT MEAN I COULD *LEAVE* IF I WANTED TO?

SURE.

OH.

ARE YOU UH GOING TO? UH GO AWAY?

I *CAN'T* LEAVE HER. SHE'S MY ONLY FRIEND. SHE DOESN'T TREAT ME LIKE A FREAK, OR A WEIRDZO, OR ANYTHING. JUST A FRIEND.

I'VE *GOT* TO STAY WITH HER, EVEN IF I DON'T UNDERSTAND THIS STUFF, AND THE BITS I *DO* UNDERSTAND SCARE ME *SHITLESS.*

THESSALY AND THE GUYS. ARE THEY *THERE* WITH HER? IN HER DREAM?

I UH DON'T THINK SO. NOT YET. THEY'RE STILL WALKING THE MOON'S ROAD.

BUT YOU SHOULDN'T WORRY ABOUT THEM...

...YOU SHOULD WORRY ABOUT *BARBIE.*

AND THE WEATHER.

I'M *HUNGRY*, WILKINSON.

Don't you WORRY, Princess. When Luz comes back she'll bring food. AND friends.

Just you keep smilin'.

Well, that everything's gone *right*. I mean, what happened to Prinado was horrible. But we still found the path, and got out of the woods.

PRINADO'S *DEAD*. I DON'T KNOW WHAT I HAVE TO SMILE ABOUT.

The Black Guard missed us in the snow, didn't they?

That's *more* than *luck*. Someone's looking out for us. I daresay when we get to the *island* something'll tell us how to use the Porpentine.

There'll be some mad old hermit. Or instructions carved on a rock, only visible on the day we get there.

It's all working out.

SHH! SOMEONE'S COMING!

Princess Barbara? Wilkinson? Are you there?

Course we're here, you great 'nana.

Well? How'd it go? Did you make contact with the *resistance*? Did you bring back any *friends*?

Yes.

Lots of them.

That's her.

Run, Princess! Get away from here!

Luz?

If you want her, you'll have to take me first!

For Murphy's sake, lass, get back into the *forest.*

RUN!

That's it. Manacle her arms. No need to bind her legs. Not yet.

But I want one of you on each side of her on the walk down.

She is not going to throw herself off the cliffs.

End of Chapter Four.

a game of you

chapter five

THE LAND.

POPPA WAS SO PROUD OF THIS LITTLE FISH.

THIRD PRIZE
1967 BASS FISHING
TOURNAMENT

IT WAS THE ONLY THING HE EVER WON A PRIZE FOR.

THIS ISN'T ANY CITADEL OF THE CUCKOO. THIS IS WHERE I GREW UP. THIS IS OUR OLD HOUSE.

IT'S JUST LIKE I REMEMBER IT, ONLY SMALLER...

AND THE BRIGHTLY SHINING SEA ISN'T ANY BRIGHTLY SHINING SEA.

IT'S THE ATLANTIC OCEAN, EARLY IN THE MORNING, AFTER THE SUN'S BURNED THE CLOUDS AWAY AND BEFORE IT'S RISEN TOO HIGH IN THE SKY, AT THE MOMENT WHEN THE SUNLIGHT TURNS THE SEA TO SILVER.

DAPPLED, GLINTING, MAGICAL SILVER...

AS IF THE LIGHT WASN'T REFLECTED; RATHER AS IF THE SEA SHONE WITH ITS OWN WONDERFUL LIGHT, GLITTERING AND SPARKLING LIKE LIQUID DIAMONDS...

WHEN I WAS A LITTLE GIRL I USED TO RUN DOWN THE SAND AND INTO THE SEA, AND I'D TRY TO PICK UP THE SHINING SILVER WATER.

I'D CUP MY HANDS AND CATCH IT, BUT IT ALWAYS TURNED BACK INTO DIRTY GRAY-GREEN SEA-WATER...

YOU'RE *ME*.

NOT *QUITE*. I'M PART OF YOU. SORT OF. YOU CREATED ME. KIND OF.

I'M THE CUCKOO.

Written by Neil Gaiman, art by Shawn McManus; additional art by Bryan Talbot and Stan Woch, colored by Daniel Vozzo, lettered by Todd Klein, edited by Karen Berger, assisted by Alisa Kwitney.

SANDMAN features characters created by Gaiman, Kieth and Dringenberg.

5: Over the Sea to Sky

BUT...

YOU--*YOU* MADE THEM KILL WILKINSON. YOU WERE THE ONE WHO DID ALL THOSE THINGS.

IT'S BECAUSE OF *YOU* MARTIN TENBONES IS DEAD.

BECAUSE OF US, PRINCESS BARBARA.

BECAUSE OF *US*.

LIKE I SAID: I'M ALMOST YOU.

WHAT *IS* THIS? SOME KIND OF MOMENT OF REVELATION? LIKE IN THE BOOKS?

IS THIS WHERE I FIND OUT I WAS ABUSED AS A CHILD AND I'VE BEEN BLOCKING IT ALL THESE YEARS?

IS *THAT* WHAT YOU ARE?

YOU WEREN'T ABUSED AS A CHILD, BARBARA. YOUR CHILDHOOD WAS DULL, QUIET AND BORING. YOU HAD TWO DULL PARENTS, AND A DULL HOUSE.

AND AN OVERACTIVE IMAGINATION.

THAT WORRIED YOUR PARENTS.

YOU'D MAKE UP STORIES, SEEK OUT BOOKS OF WITCHES AND GHOSTS -- THINGS THAT JUST WEREN'T *TRUE*. THEY COULDN'T UNDERSTAND WHERE THIS FASCINATION OF YOURS FOR THE FANTASTIC CAME FROM AND IT *SCARED* THEM.

SO YOU BEGAN TO *DEFEND* YOURSELF.

BOYS AND GIRLS ARE DIFFERENT, YOU KNOW THAT?

LITTLE BOYS HAVE FANTASIES IN WHICH THEY'RE FASTER, OR SMARTER, OR ABLE TO FLY.

WHERE THEY HIDE THEIR FACES IN SECRET IDENTITIES, AND LISTEN TO THE PEOPLE WHO DESPISE THEM ADMIRING THEIR REMARKABLE DEEDS.

PATHETIC, BESPECTACLED, REJECTED PERRY PORTER IS SECRETLY *THE AMAZING SPIDER*. GAWKY, BESPECTACLED, UNLOVED CLINT CLARKE IS REALLY *HYPERMAN*. *YES?*

WHAT HAS *THIS* GOT TO DO WITH--?

SHUSH.

NOW, LITTLE **GIRLS**, ON THE OTHER HAND, HAVE DIFFERENT FANTASIES. MUCH LESS CONVOLUTED. THEIR PARENTS ARE NOT THEIR PARENTS. THEIR LIVES ARE NOT THEIR LIVES.

THEY ARE **PRINCESSES**.

LOST PRINCESSES FROM DISTANT LANDS.

AND ONE DAY THE KING AND QUEEN, THEIR **REAL** PARENTS, WILL TAKE THEM BACK TO THEIR LAND, AND THEN THEY'LL BE HAPPY FOR EVER AND EVER.

LITTLE CUCKOOS.

DID I DREAM **THAT?** I DON'T REMEMBER ...

SURE YOU DID. YOU MADE UP A MAGIC LAND, AND YOU POPULATED IT WITH YOUR TOYS.

Barbara's ROOM

...TOYS?

YEAH. THEY'RE ALL IN HERE. IN THE SHRINE. COME ON IN.

THIS IS MY **BEDROOM**.

THAT'S RIGHT.

AND **THIS** IS MARTIN TENBONES. AND **HERE'S** WILKINSON. AND HERE'S LUZ.

HERE'S PRINADO.

HERE'S **YOU**.

TOYS. MY **TOYS**. I'D FORGOTTEN THEM.

NO YOU HADN'T. NOT DEEP DOWN. AND THEY **NEVER** FORGOT YOU.

IS THIS REAL? OR IS IT JUST MY IMAGINATION?

IF YOU TELL ME WHAT THE DIFFERENCE IS, I MIGHT BE ABLE TO TELL YOU.

I...

I WANT A DRINK OF WATER.

WELL, YOU LEFT YOURSELF WIDE OPEN FOR ME, REALLY. I MEAN, REALLY.

IT'S A LITTLE LIKE POSSESSION. ONLY I DIDN'T BOTHER WITH YOUR *BODY*.

I MOVED INTO YOUR DREAMWORLD. INTO THOSE PARTS OF YOUR LIFE YOU WEREN'T USING. YOU WERE EVERY-THING I NEEDED.

I'M YOUR IMAGINARY FIEND.

SO, BARBIE. NOW THAT I'VE EXPLAINED IT TO YOU, IT ALL MAKES PERFECT SENSE, DOESN'T IT?

...SURE.

NOW, THINK CAREFULLY BECAUSE THIS IS A *BIG* THING I'M ASKING YOU.

DO YOU *LIKE* ME?

MM HM.

AND I'VE GOT A *RIGHT* TO *LIVE*, HAVEN'T I? AND TO BE *HAPPY*?

OF COURSE YOU HAVE...

AND I'M AWFUL SWEET, AREN'T I? I'M *AWFUL* CUTE.

YOU'RE... CUTE... AS A...

...BUTTON...

BARBIE...YOU WOULDN'T *MIND* IT, IF I HAD TO KILL YOU? I MEAN COMPLETELY DESTROY YOU?

I *NEED* TO. AND IT WOULD MAKE ME *REALLY* HAPPY.

...SURE...

OH GOOD.

EVERY- THING'S FINE.

IT WAS EASY.

I WANT HER TAKEN DOWN TO THE ISLE OF THORNS.

WE START AT MOONRISE.

IDENTITY BLURS ON THE MOON'S ROAD.

I AM HAZEL McNAMARA.

I AM THESSALY.

I AM DONNA CAVANAGH.

I AM FOXGLOVE.

I AM JOHNNY McNAMARA'S BIG SISTER.

I AM A WITCH-WOMAN OF THE LOWLANDS.

I AM JUDY'S EX-LOVER.

I AM...

I...

IN THE PALE LIGHT OF THE MOON I PLAY THE GAME OF YOU.

WHOEVER I AM. WHOEVER YOU ARE.

ALL SENSE OF WHERE I AM, OF WHO I AM AND WHERE I'M GOING, HAS BEEN SWALLOWED BY THE DARK.

AND I WALK THROUGH THE STARS AND SKY...

A TRINITY OF DREAMS BENEATH THE MOON.

WHERE AM I?

WE... WHERE ARE WE?

WE ARE...

WE ARE.

WE ARE IN A *DREAM*.

AN OLD DREAM, I'D SAY--IT'S VERY SOLID.

WE'RE IN BARBIE'S DREAM?

I SUPPOSE...

IT'S MUCH OLDER THAN BARBIE, THOUGH. MY GUESS IS THAT IT'S SOMEWHERE SHE COMES TO DREAM, BUT I DOUBT SHE CREATED IT.

OW DO YOU *KNOW* ALL THIS STUFF, THESSALY?

YEAH? HOW OLD *ARE* YOU?

I'M OLDER THAN I LOOK, FOXGLOVE. YOU PICK STUFF UP AS YOU GO ALONG. YOU KNOW.

I'M REALLY PRETTY OLD. LET'S LEAVE IT THERE, HUH?

SO, WELL, NOW WE'RE HERE, WE'D BETTER START LOOKING FOR BARBIE.

THE *CUCKOO.* WE FIND THE CUCKOO.

BUT BARBIE...

BARBIE DIDN'T TRY TO HURT ME. THE CUCKOO *DID.* I'M HERE TO FIND THE CUCKOO.

I'M SURE WE'LL RUN INTO BARBIE ALONG THE WAY. THAT'S HOW THESE THINGS USUALLY SEEM TO WORK OUT. BUT *I'M* LOOKING FOR THE CUCKOO.

IT NEEDS TO BE TAUGHT A LESSON.

BUT, THESSALY...

WE DON'T *NEED* TO KNOW WHERE WE'RE GOING. THIS IS A DREAM-WORLD, FOXGLOVE. IT HAS ITS OWN LAWS, ITS OWN LOGIC. IT *NEEDS* TO BRING US TOGETHER.

UH-UH.

BUT THERE'S SOMETHING ELSE...

HAZEL? WHAT'S THE MATTER?

IT'S A *BODY*. SOME SORT OF GIANT RAT, IN A... UM. RAINCOAT.

IT'S NOT BEEN DEAD LONG.

GOOD.

IT CAN GIVE US DIRECTIONS

YOU--YOU AREN'T GOING TO CUT ITS *FACE* OFF, ARE YOU?

NO. NO NEED. BUT I'LL NEED SOME PEBBLES.

PEBBLES?

MM-HM. ROUNDISH ONES.

THERE.

NOW WE NEED A LITTLE BLOOD.

DON'T *WORRY*-- IT'LL BE MINE.

WHAT A *SWEET* LITTLE GUY. *LOTS* NICER THAN GEORGE.

MM. WHAT DO YOU KNOW ABOUT CUCKOOS?

THEY'RE BIRDS.

YEAH.

THAT'S *ALL?*

SOME CUCKOOS LAY THEIR EGGS IN OTHER BIRDS' NESTS.

SO?

THEY JUST *DO.* THAT'S ALL.

YOU *ARE* PREGNANT, AREN'T YOU?

WELL I HAVEN'T DONE A TEST OR ANYTHING. I MEAN, I DIDN'T GET ROUND TO IT YET. NOT THAT I'M WORRIED ABOUT KILLING RABBITS BECAUSE YOU DON'T HAVE TO DO THAT ANYMORE--

HAZEL. SHUT THE HELL UP.

SORRY.

SHITHEAD.

IF WE **EVER** GET HOME AGAIN, I'M GOING TO, I DON'T KNOW. **SCREAM** AT YOU. THROW THINGS ACROSS THE ROOM. I'M GOING TO CALL YOU NAMES YOU NEVER EVEN **KNEW** I KNEW...

I'M SORRY...

WHAT **KIND** OF RELATIONSHIP DID WE **HAVE**, FOR CHRISSAKES?

YOU'RE **DUMB**, YOU KNOW THAT? DUMB AND SELFISH AND, AND, DECEITFUL, AND--AND--AND-- **DUMB**.

OH...

SHIT.

DO YOU KNOW HOW MUCH A BABY'S GOING TO **COST** US?

snf?

FOR A START, WE HAVE TO BUY ONE OF THOSE DUMB BOOKS FULL OF NAMES...

FOX?

FOX, I **DO** LOVE YOU.

DAMN STRAIGHT YOU DO. **JERK**.

"IT'S JUST GOIN' TO GET WORSE."

"WELL, LUZ, NOT MUCH LONGER NOW."

"No, my lady."

"DOES THAT MAKE YOU HAPPY?"

"Very happy, my lady."

"BECAUSE YOU WANT TO PROTECT ME. YOU WANT TO HELP ME. YOU WANT TO MAKE ME HAPPY."

"Yes, lady."

IT'S TIME FOR ME TO FLY THE NEST. EVERYONE HAS TO GROW UP **SOME** TIME...

I'LL MISS THIS LAND. I REALLY **WILL**. IT'S A NICE PLACE.

WILL YOU, LUZ? THAT'S SWEET.

We'll miss you too, lady.

ESPECIALLY SINCE YOU'VE SPENT THE LAST HALF DOZEN YEARS PLOTTING MY DOWNFALL...

I was misguided, lady.

OF **COURSE** YOU WERE. AND IT JUST TOOK A LITTLE TALK TO SHOW YOU THE ERROR OF YOUR WAYS.

MMPH.

"INDEED A BIRD WILL BROOD THE FOSTER-CHICK WHILST HER OWN INFANTS LIE SLOWLY DYING OUTSIDE THE NEST..."

SHE **NEVER** UNDERSTOOD. SHE KEPT TRYING TO TELL HERSELF THE TRUTH, AND SHE **NEVER** LISTENED.

THEY DIVIDE THEMSELVES UP INTO SUCH COMPLEX PUZZLES, LITTLE BIRD...

SHE WAS THE PERFECT ENVIRONMENT TO GROW IN...

BUT WE **CANNOT** BE CHILDREN FOREVER. ALL GOOD THINGS MUST END...

AND HERE IS WHERE THEY STOP, IN THE ISLE OF THORNS...

AT THE PLACE OF THE HIEROGRAM.

AT MOONRISE. VERY *VERY* SOON.

DID YOU EVER MEET THE HIEROMANCER, LUZ?

NO, LADY.

SWEET OLD GUY. I THINK BARBIE MAY HAVE BASED HIM ON HER GRANDFATHER, WHEN SHE POPULATED THE LAND.

HE UNDERSTOOD THE HIEROGRAM.

IT'S OLDER THAN BARBIE. MUCH OLDER... IT'S OLD AS THE LAND.

THERE MUST BE *HUNDREDS* OF THESE LANDS, LITTLE BIRD. *THOUSANDS* OF THEM. AN ARCHIPELAGO OF DREAM-ISLANDS-- A GLITTERING SHOAL OF WORLDS.

COME ON, COME ON....*SET*, DAMN YOU...

LITTLE BARBIE FOUND THE LAND SHE NEEDED... AND THE LAND FOUND *SOMEONE* TO BELIEVE IN IT...

AND THEN *I* HAD TO COME ALONG AND SPOIL EVERYTHING.

OR THAT'S WHAT THE HIEROMANCER CLAIMED, WHEN I PUT HIM TO THE QUESTION.

BUT IT'S NOT IMPORTANT WHAT THE LAND IS. ONLY HOW TO LEAVE IT. I'M READY TO LEAVE THE NEST.

YOU DON'T KNOW WHAT IT'S *LIKE* TO BE PHYSICALLY CONFINED TO ONE TINY PLACE WHEN THERE ARE SO MANY *OTHER* PLACES I COULD BE...

THERE ARE *REAL* WORLDS OUT THERE: LITTLE ONES, LIKE THE ONE BARBIE INHABITS WHEN SHE'S AWAKE, AND HUGE, MARVELOUS WORLDS BEYOND *THEM*...

I'M CONSTRICTED HERE, LUZ.

I NEED TO *FLY*.

BUT I'M STUCK HERE, UNTIL THE END OF THIS WORLD. IN A WAY, I'M PLEASED THAT THE GEORGE AND THE SENDINGS FAILED SO MISERABLY.

IT WILL BE SO MUCH MORE SATISFYING TO DESTROY THE PORPENTINE MYSELF. AND THIS *IS* THE PLACE TO DO IT...

THE HIEROMANCER KNEW. KNEW A *LITTLE*. AND HE TOLD ME EVERY-THING HE KNEW, BEFORE HE DIED...

WELL, NOW IT'S JUST YOU AND ME, LITTLE BIRD LUZ.

Murphy be praised, lady-- I only live to serve you.

YES. YOU DO. AND NOT FOR MUCH LONGER.

My lady? We have guests.

THESSALY? UM, THESSALY?

ARE YOU *SURE* THIS IS THE RIGHT PLACE?

THESSALY?

I'M SURE.

HELP! PLEASE! HELP ME!

OH, I'M SO PLEASED YOU'RE HERE!

IT'S *TERRIBLE!* THE CUCKOO'S GOT PRINCESS BARBIE!

LOOK-- THEY'RE OVER *THERE.*

IT SAID IT WANTED TO *KILL* US. *PLEASE HELP ME.* SAVE THE PRINCESS.

SO *YOU'RE* THE CUCKOO, THEN?

...YES.

THESSALY?

WHY DID YOU DO THAT? JUST KILL HER LIKE THAT?

SHE NEEDED TO BE TAUGHT A LESSON.

BUT YOU JUST *KILLED* HER.

YES. *THAT* WAS THE LESSON. YOU *DON'T* GET A SECOND CHANCE.

ANYWAY, IF SHE WAS THE KIND OF THING I *THINK* SHE WAS, YOU DON'T *WANT* TO TALK TO THEM, OR LET *THEM* TALK TO YOU.

REALLY?

JUST A FEW SECONDS IS ALL THEY NEED.

YOU'RE *VERY* CLEVER. YOU REALLY ARE. YOU'RE A VERY CLEVER LADY.

BUT THAT'S *ALL* THE KILLING YOU'RE GOING TO DO, ISN'T IT?

YES.

HMM. WHAT KIND OF THING *ARE* YOU? I'VE MET THE FOLK OF THE LAND, AND A FEW PEOPLE LIKE GEORGE WHO TRAVELLED HERE IN THEIR DREAMS. AND PEOPLE FROM BARBIE'S MEMORIES.

YOU DON'T FIT.

NO.

NO MATTER.

YOU PEOPLE ARE SO *WONDERFUL*, SO JOYOUS AND STRANGE. YOU HAVE SECRET WORLDS *INSIDE* YOU. IS IT THAT WAY WITH *ALL* OF YOU?

I THINK YOU THREE SHOULD SIT DOWN NOW, AND NOT MAKE ANY MORE NOISE.

BARBIE? IT'S MOON RISE.

IT'S TIME FOR YOU TO WAKE UP NOW. COME ON.

WHU... WHERE AM I?

THIS IS THE ISLE OF THORNS.

THIS IS WHERE I HAD TO COME WITH THE PORPENTINE, ISN'T IT?

THAT'S RIGHT.

THE HIEROGRAM AND THE PORPENTINE WERE LEFT AS... TOKENS, I THINK... MANY, MANY YEARS AGO. WHILE THEY EXIST, THE LAND STILL LIVES.

THE DESTRUCTION OF *EITHER* OF THEM SIGNALS THE DEATH OF THE LAND...

THE DESTRUCTION OF BOTH *ENSURES* IT.

AND THEN I GET TO LEAVE THE *NEST*.

AND THEN I GET TO *FLY*.

I *WON!* LALLY LALLY...

I WON! I *KNEW* I WOULD.

I'M THE *CLEVEREST* AND THE *PRETTIEST,* AND ONE DAY I'LL BE THE *BIGGEST* AND THE *BRIGHTEST,* AND I'LL FLY INTO LITTLE GIRLS' MINDS AND LAY EGGS OF MY *OWN* THERE...

I WON!

I BEAT *ALL* OF YOU! LALLY, LALLY LALLY...

I CAN *LEAVE* SOON. THE PORPENTINE AND THE HIEROGRAM ARE BROKEN. THE LAND IS OVER.

NOW IT STARTS.

AND ONCE THE LAND'S GONE, LALLY, LALLY... I FLY...

OUT OF YOUR *DREAMS* INTO YOUR LIVES...

I'LL BE *BIG* AND *BEAUTIFUL* AND LAY *HUNDREDS* OF EGGS IN *HUNDREDS* OF WORLDS.

LOOK, BARBIE. *LOOK,* YOU THREE. ISN'T IT *WONDERFUL?*

THE STARS ARE FALLING.

UH-OH.

THAT WAS NEW YORK'S OWN LOU REED WITH "SATELLITE OF LOVE," BRINGING US TO A QUARTER OF FIVE IN THE MORNING.

AND WHILE IT WAS PLAYING A WEATHER FLASH CAME THROUGH, HERE ON *WRAT*. SEEMS I OWE AN EARLIER CALLER AN APOLOGY.

HURRICANE LISA--THAT'S LISA WITH AN "S"--IS *INDEED* HEADING BACK THIS WAY. THE FLASH DESCRIBES THE HURRICANE'S CHANGE OF DIRECTION AS "INEXPLICABLE."

SAYS HERE THE HURRICANE'S CHANGE OF DIRECTION MAY BE DUE IN PART TO SOME PERTURBATIONS IN THE UPPER ATMOSPHERE. METEOROLOGISTS ALSO POINT TO A POSSIBLE HIGH ALTITUDE DUST STORM WHICH HID THE FACE OF THE MOON EARLIER THIS MORNING...

MY ADVICE? STAY *HOME.* BARBARA WONG, *WRAT.*

HEY BILL?

YEAH JERRY.

YOU GOT ANY Q-TIPS ON YA?

The time has come, then.

I am here, by the terms of the compact.

Who summoned me? Who calls this skerry to its final judgment?

Who seeks my boon?

WHO ARE YOU? WHAT ARE YOU DOING HERE?

A strange question-- did you not call me, young lady?

I was your land's creator.

No, I see she did not summon me.

You did.

Hmm. You are not entirely in control of your own mind...

One moment.

I trust that feels better.

Fox? Hazel?

Thessaly?

WHAT ARE *YOU* DOING HERE?

They cannot answer you.

There.

UM...EXCUSE ME. THE PEOPLE I MET HERE KEPT TALKING ABOUT SOMEONE CALLED *MURPHY.* IS THAT *YOU*?

Indeed.

MORPHEUS. MURPHY. HM. YES.

I WOULD HAVE FIGURED THAT OUT.

BARBIE? ARE YOU OKAY? WE CAME TO *RESCUE* YOU.

Hush now. I need silence from all of you, while I do uncreate this land.

It is an old land, and it is time for it to rest.

HE BEGAN TO TALK, VERY QUIETLY, IN THAT STRANGE VOICE OF HIS, THAT SOUNDED LIKE YOU WERE HEARING IT IN THE BACK OF YOUR HEAD.

I'D HEARD THE PEOPLE TALK ABOUT MURPHY BEFORE, BUT I'D NEVER IMAGINED HE EXISTED.

IT WAS LIKE MEETING GOD, OR SOMEONE LIKE THAT. YOU DON'T FIGURE THEY'RE EVER ACTUALLY GOING TO SHOW UP.

HE WAS VERY TALL, AND VERY BEAUTIFUL, AND VERY DISTANT.

I DON'T KNOW WHAT LANGUAGE THE WORDS WERE IN, BUT I FELT LIKE I OUGHT TO HAVE UNDERSTOOD THEM-- OR RATHER, THAT PART OF ME *DID* UNDERSTAND THEM, ON SOME DEEP, BURIED LEVEL.

HIS CLOAK WAS BLOWING IN THE WIND LIKE A PATCH OF MIDNIGHT, AND HIS EYES GLITTERED LIKE TWIN STARS.

HE SEEMED TO FILL THE WORLD.

NOTHING HAD CHANGED, BUT IT WAS AS IF HE WERE AS BIG AS THE LAND, AND STILL HE WAS SPEAKING. I KNEW THAT IF HE HAD BEEN SPEAKING TO ME I WOULD HAVE UNDERSTOOD...

BUT HE WASN'T SPEAKING TO ME. HE WAS TALKING TO LUZ.

POOR DEAD LUZ, MY LITTLE JUDAS.

I COULD NOT FIND IT IN MY HEART TO BLAME HER: I, TOO, HAD BEEN ONE OF THE SERVANTS OF THE CUCKOO, FELT THE OVERPOWERING NEED TO PROTECT AND NURTURE HER; TO DO ANYTHING THAT WOULD MAKE HER HAPPY.

LUZ GOT UP.

SHE STUMBLED. AND THEN SHE WALKED INTO THE BLACKNESS OF HIS ROBE AND SHE WAS GONE.

MURPHY'S PEACE BE WITH YOU, LUZ. IF HE HAS PEACE TO GIVE.

HE CONTINUED TALKING.

AND THEY CAME.

HUNDREDS OF THEM. THOUSANDS OF THEM. WALKING AND MARCHING, SOME OF THEM DANCING DOWN THE CAUSEWAY TOWARD THE ISLE OF THORNS.

THERE WERE GIANTS AND CENTAURS AND WITCHES AND FAUNS; BEARS AND TROLLS; EVEN A HANDFUL OF GIANT SPIDERS. I SAW WILKINSON AND PRINADO, WALKING TOGETHER. THEY WAVED WHEN THEY SAW ME.

THEY WALKED PAST ME, THE LIVING AND THE DEAD, AND ONE BY ONE THEY VANISHED INTO THE DARKNESS OF HIS CLOAK.

THEN THERE WERE OTHERS WALKING PAST. DIFFERENT WONDERFUL CHARACTERS -- SOLDIERS AND COURTIERS, YOUNGEST SONS AND CATS-IN-BOOTS: THESE WEREN'T THE INHABITANTS OF MY LAND.

THESE WERE SOMEONE ELSE'S PEOPLE-- SOME EARLIER PRINCESS'S ESCAPE FROM REALITY...

DID HE BECOME HUGE?

OR DID THEY BECOME TINY AS THEY REACHED HIM?

DID SUCH CONCEPTS EVEN APPLY?

THE LAST ONE WAS THE SADDEST.

SHE WAS MAGNIFICENT. SHE LOOKED VERY PROUD AND VERY SAD. AND WHEN SHE GOT TO HIM, SHE HESITATED.

I am here, Alianora. By the terms of the compact.

I SEE. AND WHAT NOW?

Now it ends.

HOW LONG HAS IT BEEN?

A long time, old love. Your land has been home to many since your day.

SHE CURTSIED TO HIM, HE BOWED TO HER, AND SHE WAS GONE.

AND THEN HE REACHED OUT HIS HAND AND PICKED UP THE LAND.

I DON'T KNOW HOW...

IT WAS LIKE A LITTLE JEWELLED WORLD.

IT DIDN'T MATTER THAT IT WAS TINY-- IF IT *WAS* TINY. I COULD SEE EVERY WATERFALL AND STREAM, EVERY LEAF ON EVERY TREE.

I COULD SEE EVERYTHING.

AND THEN IT CRUMBLED IN HIS HAND.

IT WAS JUST DUST...

SAND,...

A GLITTERING, MULTICOLORED SAND THAT FELL AWAY INTO THE CHILLY WIND AT THE END OF THE WORLD.

THERE WAS NOTHING LEFT OF MY LAND ANYMORE--A DEAD SKY WENT ON FOREVER ABOVE US AND BELOW.

IT WAS OVER.

HE STOOD THERE IN SILENCE, LOOKING VERY TIRED, VERY ALONE. I FELT REALLY SORRY FOR HIM AND I DIDN'T KNOW WHY.

UM. ARE YOU OKAY?

Endings are mixed blessings, Princess Barbara.

But, yes, I am okay. I thank you for asking.

There. Half the compact is discharged.

Now.

I wonder if you three know the trouble you've caused.

Hmm, I know YOU, do I not?

I DON'T BELIEVE SO.

I do.

Yes. We have met before, witch woman.

IT WAS A LONG TIME AGO, DREAM KING. I'M SURPRISED YOU REMEMBER.

There were more of you then.

YES. NOW IT'S ONLY ME.

Why aren't you dead?

OH, LOOK, DON'T YOU START. IT'S A LONG STORY, AND I DON'T REALLY WANT TO GO INTO IT.

I see.

DREAM KING. THAT ONE THERE IS MY LEGITIMATE PREY-- SHE WHO CALLS HERSELF THE CUCKOO.

SHE ATTEMPTED TO HARM ME. HER LIFE IS MINE.

No, her life is her own.

SHE WOULD HAVE HARMED ME, MORPHEUS. I DEMAND MY RIGHTS.

You DEMAND?

Thessalian. The moor has tumbled into the sea, in this place. It cannot take you or you followers back to the waking world.

You are a trespasser, here without my consent.

I am very displeased.

WHAT'S HE SAYING, THESS?

I am saying, young lady, that you are here entirely--

HE'S SAYING WE'RE IN TROUBLE.

REAL TROUBLE?

Yes. Real trouble.

But then, you are far from alone in that...

UH MISS WANDA?

HI GEORGE. YOU'RE TALKING AGAIN, THEN?

YOU MAKE HIM HOLD HIS *TONGUE*, LADY. HE AIN'T A NATURAL THING.

IF SHE UH WANTED ME TO UH HOLD MY TONGUE THEN SHE'D HAVE TO DO IT FOR ME BECAUSE I DON'T HAVE ANY HANDS.

THAT'S KIND OF MY UH SORT OF *JOKE*.

THAT'S RIGHT, GEORGE.

IT DIFFERS FROM THE *USUAL* KIND OF JOKE ONLY IN THE VAST GULF BETWEEN IT AND ANY KIND OF A SENSE OF HUMOR.

SO WHAT'S *HAPPENING?*

IF YOU'RE UH GOING TO BE UH *MEAN* TO ME I UH WON'T TELL YOU.

I'M SORRY, GEORGE. TELL US *WHAT?*

UH WELL, ABOUT THE REALLY HEAVY STUFF. IT'S UH ALL REALLY GETTING BAD NOW.

I UH CAN'T FEEL THE LAND ANY MORE. OR THE UH CUCKOO. IT'S ALL MOVED AWAY.

WHAT ABOUT *BARBIE?* AND FOX AND HAZEL?

MAYBE THEY'RE *DEAD.* I UH DON'T REALLY KNOW. THEY'VE UH GONE.

JESUS WEPT. *YEAH.* THAT'S BAD STUFF, ALL RIGHT.

THAT'S UH NOT THE *REALLY BAD STUFF.*

THE REALLY BAD STUFF IS THE UH *STORM.* IT'S NOT JUST A STORM ANY MORE.

AND UH THIS IS A PRETTY *OLD* BUILDING.

GEORGE, *WHAT* ARE YOU TRYING TO SAY?

LADY...

End of Chapter Five

a game of you

chapter six

...ENTY MINUTES BEFORE SHE GETS HERE, D I'M REALLY NOT LOOKING FORWARD TO THIS.

PART OF ME IS SCREAMING JUST TO GET ON THE NEXT GREYHOUND BUS AND GET OUT OF HERE. BUT I'VE BEEN BUS-HOPPING FOR THREE DAYS NOW, SIXTEEN HUNDRED MILES...

I CAN'T BELIEVE THIS IS HAPPENING.

APPLY MAKE-UP. BREATHE DEEPLY.

TRY NOT TO REMEMBER.

⸸: "I Woke Up and One of Us Was Crying."

NEIL GAIMAN: WRITER
SHAWN McMANUS: PENCILS & INKS
TODD KLEIN: LETTERS
DANIEL VOZZO: COLORS
ALIGA KWITNEY: ASST. ED.
KAREN BERGER: EDITOR

FEATURING CHARACTERS CREATED BY GAIMAN, KIETH & DRINGENBERG

MISTER *MURPHY*? ARE YOU GOING TO DO ANY-THING ABOUT THE CUCKOO?

Do anything?

Saving only your boon, I have done all I came here to do, Barbara.

BUT SHE STILL HAS TO BE *STOPPED*.

WHY?

WELL, SHE'S *DANGEROUS*. SHE'S *EVIL*.

Dangerous? Perhaps.

But evil? She acts according to her nature.

Is that evil?

LISTEN. SHE WAS GOING TO *KILL ME*.

And your Thessalian friend wanted to kill her. Should I kill Thessaly for you, also?

DON'T PUSH YOUR LUCK, DREAM KING.

I DON'T.

I, UH, I THINK HE WAS JOKING, THESS.

But you played your part in the Cuckoo's deeds also, Barbara.

After all, it is your fault that she was bound to this skerry and could not leave it when her time came to fly, after the manner of her kind.

Mm. Yours and Rose Walker's, I should say.

LORD MORPHEUS?

Yes, Thessalian?

WHAT WILL HAPPEN TO THIS PLACE WE'RE STANDING ON, WHEN YOU GO, AND BARBIE GOES?

Hmm. I will leave it here for you. It would be unfai to remove it.

SO YOU'LL JUST *LEAVE* US HERE? IS *THAT* WHAT YOU'RE SAYING?

Can you give me any reason not to?

BUT. BUT. WE ONLY *CAME* HERE BECAUSE WE THOUGHT BARBIE WAS IN TROUBLE.

So you have said.

TCH.

Barbara? When I first created this land, quite some time ago, I made a compact with the woman for whom I created it.

It was...a compromise...

But she died, when her time came, and the compact remained uninvoked.

You have invoked the compact. The first half is completed -- the land's time is done -- now the final pact only remains.

You may ask a boon of me.

WHAT KIND OF A BOON?

Any boon that it is within my power to give.

CAN I ASK YOU TO *KILL* HER? THE CUCKOO?

Certainly. If that is to be your boon.

HMPH. THIS BOON OF MINE. COULD YOU REMAKE THE LAND? MAKE IT ALL *AGAIN*?

Certainly.

AND BRING *BACK* WILKINSON AND MARTIN TENBONES AND-- AND *EVERYONE* AGAIN? ALL MY *FRIENDS*?

Indeed. If you wish me to.

Well?

I DON'T KNOW. LET ME THINK.

BARBIE? TELL HIM TO ELIMINATE THE CUCKOO. I'LL GET THE REST OF US BACK HOME SOMEHOW.

TRUST ME ON THIS.

OH, SHUT *UP,* THESSALY.

I'VE *GOT* A BOON, HUH? OKAY. I'LL TAKE THE DOROTHY OPTION.

I WANT TO SEND US *ALL* HOME, ME AND HAZEL AND FOXGLOVE AND THESSALY. I WANT US BACK SAFE AND SOUND.

Very well.

DOES THAT MEAN I CAN FLY?

Yes.

THANK YOU.

GO AWAY.

THAT ONE NIGHT'S DREAM I PICK AT, SCAB-LIKE, IN MY HEAD.

MOST DREAMS VANISH AT DAY-BREAK. YOU FORGET.

NOT THIS. I DON'T FORGET...

OVER AND OVER AND OVER...

There, Barbara. She has gone, out of this dreamworld into worlds beyond your imagining or my dominion. She shall not trouble you again.

And perhaps your choice was wisest, after all.

You specified safe and sound, in your boon. Thus it will take a little time before I can send you all back.

I will take leave of you now, Barbara. I will be seeing you again; although you, for your part, are unlikely to see me.

OH. WELL.

NICE TO MEET YOU.

You two. You have been lucky. Understand me when I say that.

Little maiden, little mother. The future has strange journeys in store for both of you. But perhaps in future you should choose your travelling companions with more care.

And you. You have been foolish and unconsidered in your actions. You will hardly survive another century if you continue in this manner of behavior, lady.

I DON'T REMEMBER ASKING YOUR ADVICE, DREAM-KING.

It was freely given and well-meant.

Farewell.

I PROBABLY STILL SMELL LIKE THREE DAYS IN GREYHOUND BUSES AND STATIONS, BUT THERE'S ONLY SO MUCH YOU CAN DO WITH SOAP AND A WASHCLOTH IN THE JOHN...

NOT THAT WANDA'LL CARE, OF COURSE, BUT I DO WANT TO MAKE A GOOD IMPRESSION...

AFTER HE LEFT IT FELT LIKE WE SAT ON THE SAND FOREVER, WAITING TO WAKE UP.

HE COMES ON LIKE HE'S *SO* COOL. WHO DOES HE THINK HE'S FOOLING?

WELL, HE'S *NOT* FOOLING ME. *OH* NO.

THESS? CAN I ASK YOU A QUESTION?

SURE.

AND IT *ISN'T* EVEN AS IF HE'S GOOD-LOOKING. HE'S TOO *THIN*, FOR A START.

HOW *OLD* ARE YOU?

I WAS BORN IN THE DAY OF GREATEST DARKNESS, IN THE YEAR THE BEAR TOTEM WAS SHATTERED.

WHAT'S *THAT* SUPPOSED TO MEAN?

HAZE, LEAVE HER ALONE. SHE'S UPSET...

BUT I WASN'T...

THEN THERE WAS THAT SENSATION YOU GET ON WAKING, AS EVERYTHING MOVED FURTHER AWAY, AND I STARTED TO BECOME AWARE OF THE COLD--

--AND IN MY DREAM IT WAS WARM, AND SO I TRIED TO STAY IN MY DREAM FOREVER, BUT THE HARDER I HELD ON THE FURTHER IT SLIPPED AWAY FROM ME...

AND THEN I

AND THEN I WOKE

AND THEN I WOKE UP.

ANYWAY....

SOMEHOW, I REALLY *AM* IN KANSAS...

WHAT THE HELL IS *THAT*?

DON'T RECKON I KNOW, BUT IT CAN SIT ON *MY* FACE ANY TIME IT WANTS TO.

HEE HEE HEE!

HOO HOO HOO!

ASSHOLES.

YOU MUST BE HER. AREN'T YOU? AREN'T YOU ALVIN'S FRIEND?

ALVIN? OH. YEAH, RIGHT. YES, I'M BARBIE.

SIT DOWN. YOU MUST BE EXHAUSTED. CAN I GET YOU ANYTHING?

JUST COFFEE, PLEASE.

HMM. ARE YOU HUNGRY, CHILD?

WELL, JUST A LITTLE...

...YES.

JENNY-SUE? FETCH ME TWO *LARGE* CUPS OF COFFEE, AND TWO SLICES OF BLUEBERRY PIE. *BIG* SLICES, Y'HEAR?

YES, DORA.

NOW. WHAT'S THAT ON YOUR FACE?

IT'S A *VEIL*. I JUST DREW IT ON.

HMPH.

YOU AREN'T SOME KIND OF *WEIRDO*, ARE YOU, GIRL?

NO.

I *KNOW* THAT BOY WAS A SINNER.

BOY?

ALVIN. MY LATE NEPHEW. HOW *CLOSE* WERE YOU?

PRETTY CLOSE. SHE LIVED IN THE ROOM NEXT DOOR TO ME.

WE'D TALK A LOT. GO SHOPPING. YOU KNOW, JUST HANG OUT. *GIRL* TALK.

ISTEN, GIRL. WHEN YOU MEET ZEKIEL AND JOAN-ELLEN, WELL, HEY AREN'T BROAD-MINDED LIKE ME. YOU MAKE SURE THAT YOU TALK ABOUT THEIR *SON*.

THEY'VE BEEN HURT *ENOUGH* BY ALL THIS. YOU DON'T WANT TO MAKE THINGS *ANY* HARDER FOR THEM. YOU UNDERSTAND WHAT I'M SAYING?

MM-HMM.

IT'S FUNNY. IT'S OUT HERE YOU EXPECT TWISTERS AND FREAK WEATHER. NOT IN NEW YORK.

NO. *NOBODY* EXPECTED IT.

YOU WANT TO TALK ABOUT IT?

I...

OKAY, LADIES... *HERE'S* YOUR COFFEE.

AND *HERE'S* THE PIE.

THANK YOU.

THANKS, JENNY-SUE.

HEY. YOU A FRIEND OF *ALVIN*? THE MANN BOY?

YES.

I WAS AT HIGH SCHOOL WITH HIM. *WEIRD* KID. STILL, WE WERE ALL SORRY TO HEAR.

THANKS.

I... THE LAST TIME I SAW... YOUR NEPHEW... ALIVE... IT WAS THE NIGHT BEFORE THE STORM.

YOU SEE, I WAS *ASLEEP* WHEN IT HAPPENED. I MISSED OUT ON THE WHOLE THING-- HURRICANE AND ALL.

≶phhhhht.≶ BET IT GAVE YOU BAD DREAMS, THOUGH. WHEN *I* SLEPT THROUGH THE TWISTER WE HAD HERE A FEW YEARS BACK, I DREAMED I WAS IN THE *WAR* AND THEY WERE DROPPING BOMBS...

YES. I HAD DREAMS.

SO **THEN** WHAT?

THEN I WOKE UP, AND I WAS SOAKING WET, AND IT WAS DAY-LIGHT, AND THERE WASN'T ANY HOUSE ANYMORE. I WAS UNDER A PILE OF RUBBLE...

"YOU KNOW...WHAT WAS WEIRD WAS WHAT SAVED MY LIFE.

"THERE WAS A **WOMAN** ON TOP OF ME. SHE WAS **DEAD**. THIS LITTLE OLD WOMAN. HER NAME WAS MAISIE HILL, AND I'D NEVER MET HER BEFORE. AND SHE WAS ON **TOP** OF ME.

"SHE WAS CRUSHED BY FALLING BRICKS.

"SHE WAS **KILLED**. WANDA WAS KILLED. AND THIS GUY UPSTAIRS WAS KILLED. **GEORGE** -- THAT WAS **REALLY** NASTY. HE MUST HAVE BEEN IN THE **BATHTUB** WHEN IT HAPPENED.

"HIS WHOLE UPPER BODY WAS **COMPLETELY** MASHED UP."

POOR GUY. I MEAN, HE **WAS** KIND OF **CREEPY**, BUT HE NEVER DID ANYONE ANY **HARM**. NO ONE DESERVES TO GO LIKE THAT...

SO THEY PULLED YOU OUT OF THE WRECKAGE...

YEAH. IT WAS THE EMERGENCY SERVICE THEY WERE PRETTY GOOD. AND YOU KNOW THE FIRST THING I SAW WHEN I CAME OUT?

MY NEPHEW?

"UH-UH. A TV CAMERA. I'M FREEZING AND BRUISED AND THEY'VE PULLED THIS POOR OLD WOMAN OFF ME, AND I'M JUST NUMB INSIDE -- I'M IN **SHOCK** -- AND YOU KNOW WHAT HAPPENS?"

I'M MARY GENTIAN, VIEWERS, AND THIS IS JUST **ONE** OF THE **MANY** MANHATTAN PROPERTIES THAT WAS EFFECTIVELY **DEMOLISHED** BY LAST NIGHT'S HURRICANE -- **MEAN LISA** AS THEY'RE ALREADY CALLING HER.

BEHIND ME YOU CAN SEE--

HEY! LADY! GET YOUR FRIGGIN' **BUTT** OUT THE FRIGGIN' WAY. WE GOT TO GET THIS WOMAN TO THE **HOSPITAL**.

LISTEN, BUSTER, I HAVE A FIRST AMENDMENT RIGHT TO BROADCAST--

AND **I** HAVE A FIRST AMENDMENT RIGHT TO BUST YOUR FRIGGIN' **CHOPS** IF YOU DON'T MOVE...

AND *THAT* WAS WHEN I SAW WANDA.

ALVIN,

SHE WAS IN ONE OF THOSE BIG PLASTIC BAGS. WHAT ARE THEY CALLED? BODY BAGS? YOU COULD SEE *EVERYTHING*. SHE LOOKED LIKE SHE WAS ASLEEP. *THAT* WAS THE SCARY THING...

"I WANTED TO REACH OUT AND WAKE HER UP. I FOUND MYSELF THINKING ABOUT PLASTIC BAGS, AND HOW *DANGEROUS* IT IS TO PUT THEM OVER YOUR HEAD BECAUSE YOU CAN'T BREATHE AND YOU CAN *SUFFOCATE* AND EVERYTHING--

"--AND I THINK THAT WAS WHEN I WENT KIND OF *HYSTERICAL* BECAUSE THEY TOLD ME LATER I WAS JUST *SHOUTING* AT THEM, TELLING THEM TO GET HER *OUT* OF THE BAG AND GET SOME *CLOTHES* ON HER AND...

"AND..."

"AND..."

"AND..."

IT'S *OKAY*, HONEY.

IT'S OKAY.

CAN WE HAVE SOME MORE COFFEE OVER HERE?

I'M SORRY.

IKE I SAY. I WAS PRETTY MUCH OUT OF MY MIND BY THAT POINT.

I REMEMBER SEEING-- WELL, NO, NOT SEEING, *IMAGINING*--THIS HUGE BRIGHT ED *SLUG*, LIKE A, I DON'T KNOW, IKE SOME KIND OF TONGUE, SLITHERING THROUGH THE RUBBLE...

SO, UH, HOW ABOUT THE OTHER PEOPLE IN THE BUILDING? THEY WEREN'T HURT?

WELL, HAZEL AND FOXGLOVE-- THEY WERE TWO FRIENDS WHO LIVED UPSTAIRS FROM ME. *THEY* WERE FINE. AND THESSALY--SHE WAS ACROSS THE WAY-- I THINK *SHE* WAS FINE TOO.

THESSALY? ISN'T THAT A PLACE IN GREECE OR SOMEWHERE LIKE THAT?

MAYBE. I DON'T KNOW. WE *NEVER* TALKED MUCH.

SCARLETT--SHE OWNS THE BUILDING, AND LIVED ON THE VERY TOP FLOOR. SHE WAS VISITING SOME FRIENDS IN MAINE THAT WEEK.

SCARLETT CAME TO SEE ME IN THE HOSPITAL. SHE WAS REALLY UPSET. SHE SAYS THE INSURANCE COULD TAKE *YEARS* TO PAY UP. AND SHE WAS REALLY FOND OF WANDA.

IT MUST HAVE BEEN VERY TRAUMATIC FOR YOU.

YES.

≈*phhhhht.*≈ WELL...IT'S PROBABLY A *MERCY*. THE GOOD LORD TAKING ALVIN IN TO HIS BOSOM WHEN HE WAS READY.

OTHERWISE HE'D PROBABLY HAVE DIED UP THE LINE FROM *AIDS* OR SOMESUCH--OH, YOU DON'T HAVE TO *SAY* ANYTHING, I KNOW WHAT THAT BOY WAS LIKE.

GOD GIVES YOU A BODY, IT'S YOUR *DUTY* TO DO WELL BY IT. HE MAKES YOU A BOY, YOU DRESS IN BLUE, HE MAKES YOU A GIRL, YOU DRESS IN PINK.

YOU MUSTN'T GO TRYING TO *CHANGE* THINGS.

HOW WAS THE RIDE HERE?

SHITTY. LONG. CRAMPED.

YEAH.

C'MON, JENNY-SUE. THE *FUNERAL* WILL BE *STARTING* SOON.

YOU MISSED THE OPEN COFFIN AT HIS FOLKS' PLACE--ALVIN LOOKED PRETTY GOOD, AFTER THE MORTICIANS WERE THROUGH WITH HIM.

THEY CUT HIS HAIR AND PUT HIM IN A SUIT AND EVERYTHING.

BUT...WANDA WAS ALWAYS SO *PROUD* OF HER HAIR...

YOU GONNA BE IN TOWN LONG?

I DON'T THINK SO. I'M JUST HERE FOR THE FUNERAL.

WELL, YOU COME BACK ANY TIME YOU NEED A GOOD MEAL, AND WE'LL FATTEN YOU UP SOME.

PLEASE. DON'T UPSET THEM. IT'S *ALVIN*, OKAY?

YEAH. I SUPPOSE.

ZEKE? JOAN-ELLEN? THIS IS *BARBARA*. ALVIN'S FRIEND FROM NEW YORK.

MR. MANN.

THANK YOU FOR COMING ALL THIS WAY TO SHOW YOUR RESPECTS, GIRL. 'PRECIATE IT.

HOW DO YOU DO, MRS. MANN.

THE *HURRICANE*. IT WAS GOD'S JUDGMENT ON A CITY OF *SINNERS*.

BARBARA? THE SERVICE IS STARTING.

WHY DON'T YOU STAND AT THE BACK?

DORA -- WHAT'S THAT SHE'S DONE TO HER FACE?

PAINTED A VEIL ON, ZEKE. THAT'S WHAT THEY ALL DO IN NEW YORK.

DORA -- I DON'T WANT THAT GIRL COMING BACK TO THE HOUSE FOR COFFEE AND CAKES AFTERWARDS, WHAT WITH THE PEOPLE WE'VE GOT COMING OVER.

THIS TOWN'S GOING TO REMEMBER ALVIN AS THE GOD-FEARING CHILD THAT HE SHOULD HAVE BEEN.

THAT'S NOT WHAT I'D CALL HOSPITABLE, JOAN-ELLEN. SHE'S COME A LONG WAY, AND SHE'LL BE GOING BACK THIS EVENING.

WELL, I DIDN'T ASK HER.

...OR EVER THE SILVER CORD BE LOOSED, OR THE GOLDEN BOWL BE BROKEN, OR THE PITCHER BE BROKEN AT THE FOUNTAIN, OR THE WHEEL BROKEN AT THE CISTERN.

THEN SHALL THE DUST RETURN TO THE EARTH AS IT WAS: AND THE SPIRIT RETURN UNTO GOD WHO GAVE IT.

THE SERVICE DRONES TO ITS END. I REALIZE THAT I'M ALREADY BEGINNING TO FORGET WHAT WANDA LOOKED LIKE.

IS IDENTITY THAT FRAGILE?

THE THOUGHT SCARES ME.

AFTERWARD THEY PREPARE TO GO BACK TO THE MANNS' FOR COFFEE AND CAKE, AND DORA TELLS ME THEY'D RATHER I WASN'T THERE, WHICH IS FINE BY ME.

I'VE GOT A FEW THINGS TO SAY TO WANDA ON MY OWN.

DORA SAYS SHE'LL WAIT FOR ME IN THE CAR.

THEY LEAVE IN KNOTS AND CLUSTERS, AND LIKE A FLOCK OF HUGE BLACK BIRDS THEY STRUT BACK TO THEIR PICK-UP TRUCKS AND STATION-WAGONS AND HEARSES.

ALVIN
ROBERT CALEB
MANN
1966~1991

"For they have
sown the wind,
and they shall reap
the whirlwind."
HOSEA VIII, 7

WELL, YOU *REALLY DID*
IT *THIS* TIME.

MAKING ME COME
ALL THIS WAY, JUST
TO SAY *GOODBYE*.

I NEVER KNEW THAT
PLACES AROUND HERE HAD
SUCH BEAUTIFUL *NAMES*. I
WAS WATCHING THE ROAD
SIGNS FROM THE BUS.

IT GAVE
ME SOMETHING
TO DO.

CLOVERDALE, FLORISSANT,
MULBERRY GROVE, BOONVILLE, SALINA,
AURORA AND GOODLAND...

THEY SOUND LIKE
THE NAMES OF MAGIC
KINGDOMS, DON'T THEY?

YOUR AUNT
SEEMS OKAY.

WANDA?

I *WISH* YOU WERE
HERE. I MEAN, FOR A
START YOU COULD GO
SOME WAY TOWARD TELLING
ME HOW COME I WAS UP
IN GEORGE'S ROOM. *AND*
HOW COME *YOU*
WERE.

AND WHY GEORGE WAS IN
THE BATH. AND WHY FOX AND
HAZEL SEEM TO BE *AVOIDING*
ME...

...AND WHO
THE OLD LADY WAS
WHO SAVED MY
LIFE.

I MEAN, WHO *WAS* SHE, WANDA?
MAISIE HILL. I'VE NEVER EVEN HEARD
HER *NAME* BEFORE.

I WENT TO *HER*
FUNERAL LAST WEEK.
I WAS ABOUT THE
ONLY ONE THERE.

JUST ME
AND HER DAUGHTER.
THAT WAS ALL.

OH, YEAH. AND HERE...

I THOUGHT YOU'D LIKE IT. IT'S *TACKY FLAMINGO*, OR WHATEVER IT'S CALLED. YOUR FAVORITE COLOR.

WANDA

ALVIN

HEY, NO PROBLEM.

LEAST I COULD DO.

YOU *DONE*?

EVERYTHING I HAD TO DO.

WELL, GET IN, GIRL, I'LL DRIVE YOU BACK DOWN TO THE BUS STATION.

SO, WHAT ARE YOU GOING TO DO NOW?

MM. YOU KNOW WHAT MY MOM ALWAYS USED TO SAY?

SHE SAID WHEN I WAS A LITTLE GIRL I'D GO OFF AND PLAY FOR HOURS ON END.

AND WHEN SHE *ASKED* ME, SHE'D ALWAYS GET THE SAME ANSWER. "WHERE YOU BEEN?" "OUT."

"WHAT YOU BEEN DOING?" "NOTHING."

YEAH. ALL KIDS SAY THAT.

THEY *DO*? I THOUGHT IT WAS JUST *ME*.

ANYWAY, *THAT'S* WHAT I'M GOING TO DO NOW.

HOW DO YOU MEAN?

WHERE AM I *GOING*?

WHAT AM I GOING TO *DO*?

OUT.

NOTHING.

YOU SEE, I *USED* TO BE A PRINCESS. I HAD A *CUCKOO* IN MY HEAD.

OH.

WELL... ISN'T THAT NICE...

TAKE THE REST OF THE DRIVE
[BA]CK IN SILENCE. AND SUDDENLY
I'M REMEMBERING.

IT'S YESTERDAY: I'M ON A GREYHOUND BUS, DUE TO GET IN TO INDIANAPOLIS ABOUT 4:00 AM.

OUTSIDE IT'S SLUSH AND SLEET, AND INSIDE WE'RE ALL UNCOMFORTABLE AND THE MAN IN THE SEAT IN FRONT OF ME KEEPS WHISPERING, "MR. WIGGLY HASN'T GOT NO NOSE" TO HIMSELF, THEN BURSTING INTO TEARS.

[I] CAN HEAR THE SLOOSH, SLOOSH OF [TH]E WINDSHIELD WIPERS. UP UNTIL NOW, [I] HAVEN'T FELT TIRED, BUT NOW [SU]DDENLY MY CHIN BEGINS TO DIVE [DO]WNWARD, AND THE SECOND OR [THI]RD TIME THIS HAPPENS I GO WITH IT.

I DREAM OF WANDA. ONLY SHE'S PERFECT. SHE REMINDS ME OF GLINDA IN THE OZ MOVIE, SOMETHING I'M SURE SHE'D GET A HUGE KICK OUT OF HEARING.

AND WHEN I SAY PERFECT, I MEAN PERFECT. DROP-DEAD GORGEOUS. THERE'S NOTHING CAMP ABOUT HER, NOTHING ARTIFICIAL. AND SHE LOOKS HAPPY.

[W]ANDA'S WITH THIS WOMAN I DON'T KNOW. AND THE [W]OMAN GOES UP ON TIPPIE-TOE AND WHISPERS SOMETHING INTO WANDA'S EAR.

THEN WANDA TURNS AROUND AND SHE SEEMS TO SEE ME, AND SHE WAVES.

THEY BOTH WAVE.

AND I'M GOING TO WAVE BACK; BUT THE BUS PULLS INTO THE STATION, AND THEY OPEN THE DOOR, AND IT'S FREEZING, AND WE ALL GET OFF THE BUS AND TRY TO PERSUADE A BUSTED SOUP MACHINE TO GIVE US SOMETHING HOT TO DRINK...

AND IF THERE'S A MORAL THERE, I DON'T KNOW WHAT IT IS, SAVE MAYBE THAT WE SHOULD TAKE OUR GOODBYES WHENEVER WE CAN.

AND THAT'S ALL.

A BRIEF AFTERWORD

This story was written in a number of places, mostly in an office in Sussex, England, a hotel room in Wilmington, NC, and an apartment in Northampton, MA.

I couldn't and wouldn't have done it without Jonathan Carroll, who talked me into telling a story I had thought best left alone, and who taught me that one of the purposes of a writer is to write it new; the late Don Melia and his unnamed just-as-late roommate, who planted a seed that became Wanda.

Kevin Eastman gave me somewhere to hide while I was writing part of the story. Dolores Meeks and Susan Alston made sure I was fine, and Scott and Ivy McCloud took me out for ice cream.

Steve Bissette, Michael Zulli (who was there the day the story began), Rick Veitch and the rest of the Massachusetts mafia gave me support and encouragement.

On the home front I owe thanks to Mary Gaiman, our son Michael, and to Holly, our daughter, from whom I learned that cuckoos go *Lally Lally.*

My thanks to Shawn McManus, to Colleen Doran, and to Bryan Talbot (who rescued us at the last moment), and to Stan Woch, George Pratt and Dick Giordano. Todd Klein did his usual remarkable job, and Danny Vozzo made it happen in color. Karen Berger, my editor, kept editing despite having to go and give birth to Zachary Bruning in the middle (We were on the phone at the time. Honestly.); and Alisa Kwitney, assistant editor, dropped in at the deep end, did miracles.

Dave McKean is one of a kind, and it's hard to thank him enough for his vision or his friendship.

Bob Kahan brought to this collected edition the same dedication and obsession with detail he brought to *Season of Mists.* It's appreciated.

And there are other people without whom: Babs, Roz, Rachel, Ian and Anne, Patrick and Teresa, Steve Brust, Will and Emma, Steve Jones, Pete Atkins, Jim Chadwick, Tom Peyer, Jim Herbert...but that list's too long to print here and is, anyway, unfinished.

I spent more than half a year with Barbie and Wanda and Hazel and Foxglove and Wilkinson and Thessaly and the rest of them wandering around in my head.

Some nights I still miss them.

Neil Gaiman
4 March 1993

BIOGRAPHIES

NEIL GAIMAN's (writer) favorite toys were mostly books. His favorite game was to find somewhere inaccessible and out of the way, and go read there for hours. He knew that he could go to Narnia or Oz or Cimmeria or New York if he just said the right thing or rubbed the right magic charm, but it just never happened.

TODD KLEIN's (letterer) favorite book was *The Marvelous Land of Oz*. His game now is Scrabble.

SHAWN McMANUS' (artist, chapters 1, 2, 4 6) favorite book wa *Where the Wild Thing Are*. He was born o the 30th of June, 195 His best game was Tag

BRYAN TALBOT (penciller, additional art in chapter 5) had about ten imaginary friends, all called Bryan. As a child, on the seafront at Blackpool, Bryan would put his pennies into mechanical tableaux, and watch *The Opium Smoker's Nightmare*, *The Drunkard's Dream*, and *Midnight at the Graveyard*.

BOB KAHAN's (editor, collected edition) favorite book as a child was *Tom Swift and His Amazing Flying Machine*. His most vivid childhood memory is of his sister pushing his baby carriage down a flight of steps "which is really weird, because she's younger than me."

GEORGE PRATT (original inker, chapter 3) had an imaginary friend but has forgotten his name. He remembers being in the hospital in Houston to have heart surgery and watching the *Batman* TV show. At the same time he got to meet Miss America.

ALISA KWITNEY (not pictured) (assistant editor) had a security blanket called Schmatta, and two imaginary friends named Roland and Syrup. Roland got his name from a small boy in Majorca who cracked open his head running full-tilt into a wall.

DANNY VOZZO's (colorist) favorite book was *Green Eggs and Ham*. He had an imaginary friend but "he didn't last long. He kept cutting out on me. His name was Skids."

COLLEEN DORAN (artist, chapter 3) lived on a corner known as Crash Corner; one day she saw a child on a bicycle get hit by a car and fly 20 feet through the air. She was sitting in a tree in the front yard at the time. Her favorite book was *The Secret Garden* by Frances Hodgson Burnett.

DICK GIORDANO (original inker, chapter 3) was born in 1932, and maintains his favorite game is, and always has been, It. As in "Let's do it."

STAN WOCH's (inker, additional art in chapter 5) most vivid memory is of riding on his father's shoulders as he waded through a shallow inlet where stingrays were breeding.

KAREN BERGER (editor) had a Tressy doll when she was younger. Tressy was like a Barbie, but her hair grew when you pressed her stomach. She used to steal flowers from people's gardens and hide them in her closet. It was a game, like "'A' My Name Is 'Alice.'"

SAMUEL R. DELANY's (introduction) childhood can be observed in his volume of autobiography "*The Motion of Light and Water.*"

DAVE McKEAN's (covers and design) favorite toy was a woolen fish. It was called Fish. These days his favorite game is trying to get color copiers to do things they were never intended for, nor ever dreamed of doing.

THE SANDMAN VOL. 4:
SEASON OF MISTS

FROM THE NEW YORK TIMES # 1 BEST-SELLING AUTHO

NEIL GAIMAN
THE SANDMAN

The *New York Times* Best-Selling Author of
The Graveyard Book and *Coraline*

the SANDMAN

Neil Gaiman

volume 1
preludes & nocturnes

sam Kieth
mike Dringenberg
malcolm Jones III

FULLY RECOLORED EDITION